He's Listening
So Talk to Him!
A practical guide to prayer

by Paul Bunday

Please note:
All Bible quotations are from the
New Revised Standard Version
unless otherwise stated.

Abbreviations:

GNB – Good News Bible
KJV – King James Version
LB – Living Bible
NIV – New International Version
TEV – Today's English Version

Copyright © 2002 by Paul Bunday

First published in 2002

All rights reserved. No part of this publication
may be reproduced
in any form without prior
permission from the publisher.

British Library Cataloguing in Publication Data.
A catalogue record for this book is available
from the British Library.

ISBN 1-873796-98-6

Published by
AUTUMN HOUSE
Alma Park, Grantham, Lincs, England, NG31 9SL

2 4 6 8 10 9 7 5 3 1

Acknowledgements

I wish to express my deepest gratitude to my wife Cynthia, and my close friends Colin Bell and Frank Anstis, for their invaluable help in preparing this book. My thanks also to David Marshall and the staff at Autumn House for their advice and encouragement.

About the **Author**

Paul Bunday is married with three children. He was educated at Epsom College – where he was captain of the cricket XI – and Wadham College, Oxford. Following his National Service in Fighter Control, he trained for the ministry at the London College of Divinity under Dr Donald Coggan (later Archbishop of Canterbury).

Following his ordination, Paul Bunday was curate at Woking, before spending six years as Chaplain of Reed's School, Cobham. During the final years of his parochial ministry – in the Marlborough area – he developed a particular interest in biblical meditation; his book on this subject (*Spirit Borne*) was published by Bible Reading Fellowship in 1996.

Canon Bunday is now retired and lives with his wife Cynthia near Salisbury. He continues to offer a ministry in prayer and Bible meditation. His interests include walking and cricket.

Dedication

*For my children
Anthony
Jonathan
Kathryn*

Contents

1 Priority 9

2 Privilege 15

3 Preparation 23

4 Partnership 36

5 Problems 45

6 Peace 57

7 Penitence 69

8 Pleasure 79

9 Presence 88

10 Pattern 97

11 Psalms 109

12 Paul 123

13 Parables 138

14 Pathfinders 149

15 Power 158

Speak to him for he hears;
and Spirit with spirit meet.
Closer is he than breathing,
and nearer than hands or feet.
ALFRED, LORD TENNYSON (1809-1892)

Every promise of Scripture is a writing of God,
which may be placed before him with this reasonable request,
'do as thou hast said!'
The Creator will not cheat his creature who depends upon his truth;
and far more
the heavenly Father will not break his word to his own child.
C. H. SPURGEON (1834-1892)

Upfront

The Most Important Issue

'I found myself asking if there was one message from God more than any other that we needed to hear in the twenty-first century. Was there one particular aspect of Christian experience that needed to be deepened? What should be the highest priority in our personal Christian lives for the new century?

'I became increasingly convinced that there was such a theme. . . . That theme was prayer.

'As Christians we all need a deeper understanding of prayer, for what higher hope can we possibly have than to be linked with the Creator of the universe, to be able to tap his divine power? Nothing can be more pressing than that God's people should experience all the supernatural power he has available for them.'

PAUL BUNDAY, *Salisbury*

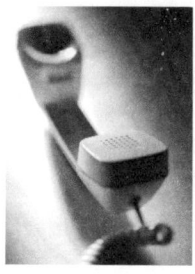

Chapter **one**

Priority

The new millennium was under way. We were witnessing its birth in Southampton; and halfway through the church's celebration party we moved outside and stood on a bridge, better to enjoy the city's fireworks as they exploded into the midnight sky.

Then, two weeks later, it was back to 'business as usual', as I settled down to prepare for the services I was due to lead. I found myself asking if there was one message from God more than any other that we needed to hear in the twenty-first century. Was there one particular aspect of Christian experience that needed to be deepened? What should be the highest priority in our personal Christian lives for the new century? It did not have to be anything new; it could just as easily be the recovery of a well-known truth that had become so commonplace it had lost its vitality. Was there any prompting by God to concentrate on some vital theme for the whole year?

I became increasingly convinced that there was such a theme, one that I ought to pursue at every opportunity afforded me in my retirement ministry. That theme was prayer. Surely, there could be no more important subject for personal consideration at the start of this millennium!

As Christians we all need a deeper understanding of prayer, for what higher hope can we possibly have than to be linked with the Creator of the universe, to be enabled to tap his divine power? I felt very clear in my own mind that nothing could be more pressing than that God's people should experience all the supernatural power he has available for them. I recalled the vision of heaven that Esther de Waal quotes in her book, *Living with Contradiction*, the picture of heaven as a vast lost-property office filled with unclaimed parcels, all having names written on them, representing all the gifts that our Father God so wants to give us, but which we have never claimed and so never enjoyed.

The tragedy is that so many of us don't know what we are missing; we just sense there is so much more. This has been borne out in my parish ministry where the pre-eminent and recurring plea has been for more help in prayer. I've little doubt

A **prayer** of seeking

> Lord, teach me to seek thee,
> and reveal thyself to me when I see thee,
> for I cannot seek thee unless thou teach me,
> nor find thee except thou reveal thyself.
> Let me seek thee in longing, let me long for thee in seeking;
> let me find thee in love, and love thee in finding.
>
> St Ambrose (c. 340-397)

that most clergy meet with the same request. I also recall an opinion poll taken by a popular Christian magazine some years ago which asked the question, 'Where do you need most help in your Christian life?' The overwhelming response was: 'In the practice of prayer'.

All that follows is the result of addressing that plea for help as I concentrated on this vital subject throughout the year. Whatever the season of the church's calendar, I have tried to introduce the subject of prayer at some point in my teaching. Frequently, it has been possible to preach about prayer as the major theme of the sermon. But, in any event, if we engage in regular worship and personal Bible study, we would do well to ask ourselves how our prayer life is being affected by what we hear and read week by week. Behind all our present experience of prayer lies the uncomfortable truth that our prayer lives show more clearly than anything else what we actually believe about God. We should put to one side what we tell others we believe about God, and try to sideline what we would like to think that we believe about him, and concentrate on an actual analysis of our own prayers. What do they tell us about our true state of faith at the moment?

It's sensible to have a medical check-up from time to time, even if we are feeling reasonably well. It is also prudent to expose ourselves to a spiritual examination on occasions. Sometimes this can be done with the help of persons we trust and who are able to question us sensitively about our spiritual lives. But, as often as not, we are diffident about exposing ourselves to scrutiny even from close friends or trusted leaders. Perhaps we sense weakness in too many areas of our Christian lives and feel threatened.

Here is a simple and totally confidential way in which you can assess your progress. Just ask yourself this question: 'What priority do I give to prayer in my life?' Be honest about the answer. Push through the various excuses that are bound to come to mind. You will find that the time factor will always be high on

A **prayer** for wisdom

> O gracious and holy Father,
> give us wisdom to perceive thee
> diligence to seek thee,
> patience to wait for thee,
> eyes to behold thee,
> a heart to meditate upon thee,
> and a life to proclaim thee.
> ST BENEDICT (C. 480-547)

the list, given the demands of family, work or social commitments. And there is always the universal experience that, although prayer sounds hugely important in theory, the moment you try to carve out a quiet space, all kinds of inner turbulence rise to the surface.

It is all too easy to give up before you've really got going, excusing yourself with the thought that you will probably feel more like it later on. Just keep pressing the question for several days; mull it over until you finally come to an accurate assessment of your position. Ask God the Holy Spirit to help you to be honest and realistic. I am not asking how successful you think your prayer life is; I just want you to see very clearly what priority you give to it in your daily timetable. Only you will know what you've discovered.

If, at the end of your personal evaluation, you feel that you wish to give a higher priority to prayer, then we can move on together. This book has been written for you. The only condition to a successful outcome is that you want to take prayer more seriously than you have in the past. Perhaps this will help to focus and refine your attitude towards prayer. And I hope you share my own conviction that however badly we do it prayer is vitally important.

In the last few minutes I have been asking some very personal questions to which only you will know the answers, because we are talking about the most secret place of the soul, where no one else has access except the Holy Spirit. Assuming that you are intending to read on, I would be fascinated to know what kinds

A **prayer** of praise

> Glory be to thee, O Christ our Prophet,
> who didst reveal and interpret thy Father's will
> and all saving truth to the world.
> Glory be to thee, O Christ our Priest,
> who didst offer thyself a sacrifice for sin
> and ever livest to make intercession for us.
> Glory be to thee, O Christ our King,
> who dost give laws to thy people
> and dost govern and protect us in thy love,
> and who reignest with the Father and the Holy Spirit,
> now and forever.
>
> *THOMAS KEN (1637-1711)*

of answers you would give, say, in about six months' time.

Whenever I have read a book on prayer, I have been grateful when the writer has divulged his or her own experiences, including the actual words that are used. I very often experiment with their ideas myself. Sometimes they work well for me and so become part of my permanent practice. At other times the new thoughts don't strike a chord and I quietly let them go. All the same, I am grateful to have tried the experiment and to know I have learned from it. I hope the same happens for you as you read on. See what really works for you, what opens doorways in your own experience. Retain all that seems good and right; quietly drop all that hasn't been helpful to you.

Hold on to the important truth that, however poorly you may think you are praying, every time you come to God in prayer you are opening yourself to the almighty Creator of the universe, who has unlimited power at his disposal.

And so no activity in life can be more important. Samuel Chadwick wrote: 'It would seem as if the biggest thing in God's universe is a man who prays. There is only one thing more amazing, and that is that man, knowing this, should not pray.' I hope I have sufficiently emphasised the point about priority.

Chapter **two**

Privilege

In the last years of his career in the Civil Service, my father became head of the Special Investigation Branch of H.M. Customs & Excise, and in line with traditional practice he was awarded the O.B.E. His invitation to Buckingham Palace for the ceremony allowed him to take two guests, and he nominated my mother and me.

We made due preparation for the great day and eventually arrived at the Palace gates. Of course, we had been there a number of times before, but only to peer through the railings. That time we were privileged to pass through into the first courtyard. For the next twenty minutes we moved through the front part of the Palace and into the inner courtyard, where the heart of the building, invisible from the Mall, came into view.

We then passed through doorways, along corridors hung with priceless works of art, through hallways, until, eventually, we took our seats in the great ballroom where the investiture would be held. The next half an hour was spent settling down and listening to a military band playing in the gallery.

When my father eventually moved forward to receive his

decoration, the Queen spoke a few words, asking him about his work, and he made a brief reply. Then it was all over.

Such preparation had been made for the day – the right dress, travel arrangements, correct procedure for entry into the Palace, the waiting period in the ballroom. And finally the great moment when little more than a dozen words were spoken by both parties. But at the heart of it had been that supreme moment when the Queen and my father had met, face to face, and talked together. What a privilege! Yet all over in thirty seconds!

Bearing this in mind but moving to a far higher sphere, I wonder if each one of us realises that he has an infinitely greater privilege than this. We are actually invited to approach the King of kings and Lord of lords, the awesome, the almighty, holy, living God at any moment of any day – and for an unlimited period of time. Through prayer, at any time of day or night, we truly have access to the Creator of the universe. We are allowed to approach the One who is omniscient and omnipresent, because he is always there waiting for us. What an amazing, almost unbelievable privilege!

Of course, no one can gain an audience with the Queen just because he wishes it. No one would even be allowed through the main gates of Buckingham Palace without the correct entry documents. All kinds of checks are made before the invitation into the Queen's presence is issued. And then the personal invitation becomes the passport for the audience.

In the same way, only at an infinitely higher level, we have no right in ourselves to claim entry into the holy presence of the living God. But as Christians we can be assured that we have privileged access to the Father of our Lord Jesus Christ. When we, in trust, commit ourselves to Jesus, it is as though he personally introduces us to almighty God and gives us access to the very throne room of heaven, where we are allowed, indeed encouraged, to converse with our heavenly Father. And this conversation is not limited to thirty seconds of rather stiff, formal words. Its duration is unlimited, certainly on God's side. And don't forget that the third Person of the Holy Trinity is the actual inspirer of our prayer relationship. It's amazing that the Holy Spirit is able to sustain all the prayer conversations that are taking place throughout the world at any given time, for prayer is a spiritual activity and God is perfect spirit.

In prayer, then, we come to the Father through the Son in the Spirit. Jesus Christ, the Son, through his death and resurrection, brings us to the Father and makes it possible for us to stand in his presence. And the Holy Spirit prompts, encourages and inspires our prayers so that in this amazing spiritual activity we are actually engaging with all members of the Trinity.

My sister recently worked in China for Voluntary Service Overseas. During the greater part of three years, she was stationed in a comprehensive school in the far north-east of the country where Mongolia was nearer than Beijing. She was the only western woman living in the town, and naturally felt very distant from her family in the UK. Letters took about twelve days to arrive; parcels rather longer, if they ever arrived at all. But the telephone link was extremely good. The combined international and local numbers ran to no fewer than fourteen digits but, having pressed all the right buttons, she made the connection swiftly, proved by the sound of the regular ringing tone; and how clearly my sister's voice came over the line! If human technology can link two people as easily as that, I have no problem with God's spiritual technology linking us immediately with him. And don't forget that the heavenly call is both instant access and freephone!

However badly we think we are praying; however difficult it is to get started, however ineffective we feel our prayers are; however stilted or formal the language; however inadequately

A **prayer** of longing

> Late have I loved you,
> O Beauty so ancient and so new.
> You called, and broke through my defences,
> and now I long for you.
> You breathed your fragrance on me,
> and I drew in my breath and now I pant for you.
> I tasted you, and now I hunger and thirst for you,
> you touched me,
> and I burn for your peace.
> ST AUGUSTINE OF HIPPO (354-430)

we think we have dealt with the various subjects that we have tried to pray about, as long as we are conscious of the incredible privilege we possess in being invited to pray at all, we shall be fulfilling one of the greatest requirements of prayer.

Taking this truth about prayer at its most basic level, if you can only just breathe the name of God, then you are linking yourself with the almighty Spirit of the universe; you are standing on the edge of what William Temple describes as 'the unsearchable abyss of eternity'.

Sometimes my prayers are no more than breathing the name

of God silently within my mind. I say the words as slowly as possible to savour the privilege of having direct access to my heavenly Father. It is good simply to wait upon him, while recognising his total reality, and being confident that when Jesus says to his followers, 'Remember, I am with you always' (Matthew 28:20), he means exactly what he says. Christ is giving us his word, he is making a promise. Come what may, God will never break his word, as he has told us, 'the mountains may depart and the hills disappear, but my kindness shall not leave you. My promise of peace for you will never be broken . . .' (Isaiah 54:10, LB). So, however sluggish or depressed we may feel, whatever difficulties we may be experiencing, Jesus Christ has promised his presence and has invited us to come to him: 'Come to me, all you who are weary and burdened, and I will give you rest' (Matthew 11:28, NIV). 'Whoever comes to me I will never drive away' (John 6:37, NIV). May I suggest that you mentally just breathe the name of God:

>Almighty holy Lord . . .
>
>Abba Father God

Jesus himself used the beautiful Aramaic word *abba* when he prayed in the Garden of Gethsemane, and the gospel has preserved it in the original language which he spoke (Mark 14:36). Also, the apostle Paul tells us to use the same word in our prayers to God (Galatians 4:6). We speak to the Father and to the Son, so breathe the name of Jesus as well:

>Lord Jesus Christ . . . Son of God . . . .

for the name of Jesus has immense spiritual power as we shall see when we consider it in greater detail later.

Prayer is not so frequently made to the Holy Spirit, but there is no good reason at all why he should not be addressed; after all he is the Paraclete, the divine Friend who pleads our cause. Actually, prayer is made to him in one of the earliest Christian Latin prayers: *Veni Spiritus Sancte* – Come Holy Spirit.

Just to breathe the title, Paraclete, which Jesus gave to the Holy Spirit, is true prayer. It implies that we are calling upon all his attributes of love, understanding and companionship, and his power to guide and protect. The holy Paraclete knows us through and through as our lives are an open book to him. He answers the attacks that come to us from the enemy within, and he stands by us at all times with encouragement and reassurance.

And so, as we invoke the name of God, the holy Trinity, we should become more conscious of the supreme privilege of prayer, for we are spiritually in the very throne room of heaven. The angelic choir is singing tirelessly and eternally in the background. Paul himself confirms that we have this glorious privilege of access to God: 'In union with Christ and through our faith in him we have the boldness to go into God's presence with all confidence' (Ephesians 3:12, GNB) and he encourages us to use it.

When I am using the names of God, the holy Trinity, in this way, I find it helpful to breathe the words as slowly as possible and to deepen my breathing rhythm slightly. This helps me to concentrate on the deep meaning of the words I am using, and assists in bringing a sense of the peace of God during prayer.

As you quietly repeat the names of God, the sense of privilege will frequently lead into the praise and adoration which are great keynotes of prayer.

William Temple has given some of the most encouraging words about adoration that I have ever encountered. They come from his commentary on John's gospel:

'Both for perplexity and for dulled conscience the remedy is the same; sincere and spiritual worship. For worship is the submission of all our nature to God. It is the quickening of conscience by his holiness; the nourishment of mind with his beauty; the opening of heart to his love; the surrender of will to his purpose – and all of this gathered up in adoration, the most self-less emotion of which our nature is capable and therefore the chief remedy for that self-centredness which is our original sin and the source of all actual sin. Yes, worship in spirit and truth is the way to the solution of perplexity and to the liberation from sin.'

We don't need to use many words to pray sincerely, and so the few we actually use, when breathed in adoration, constitute true prayer:

> Almighty holy Lord
> Abba Father God
> Lord Jesus Christ
> Son of God
> Come Holy Spirit
> Paraclete

Yes, prayer is freephone and instant access to the King of the universe. At any time and in any place God is available and we are instantly connected, and we can be absolutely sure of this at all those special times when we set aside a period in the day simply to be consciously with him. But it's also true for any moment of day or night whatever we're doing; walking or working, rushing or resting, on a train or waiting for someone to keep an appointment, or tossing restlessly during the slow night hours. At any point in time we can make contact with the God of all peace who guides and protects. We need do no more than shoot up an 'arrow prayer' or just repeat some words of Scripture and offer them to God: 'Be sure I am with you always', 'Peace I leave with you; my peace I give to you.'

And it's freephone because the God of all grace gives this priceless gift to us spontaneously; so that we can realise his presence at any moment. What an incredible privilege!

Chapter **three**

Preparation

Jesus himself gave the clearest possible advice concerning the right preparation for prayer. In the Sermon on the Mount he tells his followers, 'enter into thy closet, and when thou hast shut thy door, pray to thy Father which is in secret; and thy Father which seeth in secret shall reward thee openly' (Matthew 6:6). I have quite deliberately reverted to the old King James Version for that verse because it makes an important point. All the modern versions speak of going into 'a room' or 'your room', but I still think of going into the 'closet' as the great act of preparation for prayer.

In effect, Jesus is telling us to go into the smallest room in the house. For most Jewish families of that time, apart from the communal living-room, that would be the only other room in the home. He grew up in Nazareth in a one-roomed open-plan house, just like most other people in the village. In this one room everything happened: it was the hub of family life; the household ate, sat, talked, entertained and slept within its walls. At one end of the room would have been a raised wooden platform just under a foot high. This was where the family slept together under an odd assortment of coverings. The door of the house would be open to the street during the day and closed only at night while the family slept. This meant that friends and neighbours could come and go as they pleased, which made village life very sociable. It also meant free access for all the local animals.

Because of hygiene problems posed by this ever-open door, most Jewish homes had built on to them a very small room

A **prayer** of awareness

> Be still Silent Aware
> for there in your own heart the Spirit is at prayer.
> Listen and look
> Open and find - Christ
> *PRAYER FROM MALLING ABBEY, KENT*

where food could be kept cool and secure. This pantry is what the King James Version translates as the 'closet'. So perhaps it was in the pantry of his Nazareth home that Jesus first learned the art of mental prayer. In the noisy, bustling life of his large family, all crammed into the one room; it was the only place where Jesus could find the quietness and solitude essential for personal prayer. When I speak of 'closet' prayer, you now know what I mean.

Throughout my Christian life I have been fortunate in having access to a prayer closet. At home, and also as a college student, I enjoyed a small room to myself. As a minister in the Church of England I always had a personal study. Today, even in our small retirement house, I have a closet, not quite the smallest room in the house but a small boxroom, in which I can be alone and quiet to read and pray. I am thankful for this; for me it is vitally important.

Perhaps my most profound experience of closet prayer came when I was asked to unite three separate, distinctive and strong parishes into a new Team ministry. Although it was a wonderfully rewarding experience, I found it a very stressful time.

My rectory at first was an eight-bedroomed Edwardian house, which was due to be sold as it was very expensive to maintain. It so happened that a suitable house, directly opposite us in the road, came onto the market, and it was decided that this would be the new rectory. For about four months it stood empty, and during that time I had free access to it. There were three floors, and I quickly decided that my new study would be a small room on the top floor, which had a marvellous view over Weymouth Bay. Naturally, at that time my future study was unfurnished, but it did boast a piece of carpet left behind by the previous owners. I carried a garden chair across the road and then I had all I needed for the best experience of closet prayer that can be imagined. The house was silent, the telephone not yet connected; no doorbell rang because no one except my family knew that I was there. I could do exactly as Jesus instructed: I entered my closet, shut the door and spoke to my heavenly Father.

After the stress of life outside I was very conscious of God's peace in this room, and on one occasion I specially asked the Lord if he had a particular word for me. During the next few minutes single words seemed to form distinctly and clearly in my mind. There was an interval of perhaps a minute or so between the words which were: STOP: REST: LISTEN. For about ten minutes I allowed them to revolve around my mind and then I simply asked if there was anything more, to which the answer came: GIVE THANKS.

I sensed that God had spoken to me, but I needed to test the words in case they were merely a projection of my subconscious mind. First, did they square with Scripture? Here, I could not point to any one text where these four words were given in the sequence in which I had received them. But I could think of a number of psalms in which those four principles of prayer could be found. Again, in the personal prayer practice of Jesus, particularly as seen in John's gospel, they seemed to be exemplified. While I have to admit it is most unusual for the Lord to speak to me with such clarity, I am today in no doubt that those four words were meant for me, not least because for twenty years they have been central to my prayer experience. I should like to explore these four key words with you a little more deeply.

Stop

Jesus said that we were to go into the closet and shut the door. Inside his closet there would have been just enough room to sit down. There might well have been a small air-vent in the wall but certainly no window. Compared with the hot and bustling life outside it would have been cool and quiet inside. It would have been too dark for reading. Not that Jesus would have had anything to read, for the bulky Old Testament scrolls were kept securely in the local synagogue chest. Nor would he have needed them. Jewish boys were given six years of education at the village synagogue school until they became 'sons of the law' on their twelfth birthday. During those years the boys would be taught to understand the Old Testament while learning large parts of it by heart. And so Jesus would have memorised the laws of Moses, many of the psalms and the more important parts of the prophets. He would certainly have had immediate mental access to much Scripture as he sat quietly in meditation and prayer in the closet.

Where is your prayer 'closet'? Perhaps you have the luxury of a room where you can be alone and silent whenever you choose to STOP before God. Or perhaps your home circumstances mean that you have to find your quiet place in a spare bedroom, or choose the twenty or thirty minutes during the day when you know that one of the rooms in the house will be unoccupied. I realise that a busy mother with a young family may face a greater challenge than most of us, for even the very early morning period of quiet cannot be guaranteed with a baby or toddler in the house. But call to mind the experience of John Wesley's mother. Susannah Wesley had fourteen children but still managed to retreat into her closet. She simply sat down in her chair, picked up the bottom corners of her voluminous apron and threw it back over her head. The children knew exactly what that signified – Mother was praying. And woe betide any child who carelessly or for no good reason disturbed her!

Maybe you need to think about somewhere outside your home.

At one time I lived on the edge of the New Forest (my parish boundary was the Forest cattle-grid). I would prepare the rough notes for my Sunday sermon in my study and then drive to a quiet spot just inside the Forest. There, in the silence of the ancient hardwood trees, I shaped the message into its final form and prayed that the Holy Spirit would bring it alive on Sunday morning. And so sometimes the car can be a great place of quiet.

It sounds easy enough to say that we STOP in the presence of the Lord, but for many of us this is more difficult than it sounds. We can stop and quieten the body, but our thoughts continue to dart all over the place. So before we can stop at every level we need to slow down mentally and emotionally. We should relax our bodies as far as we can. If we are conscious of tension in

A **prayer** of silence

> All voices must have become dumb
> to him who would hear God's whisper.
> MEISTER ECKHART

arms, legs or neck, we should flex and release the muscles a number of times, deepen our breathing and use our imaginations to picture Jesus Christ speaking to us:

Be still in my presence

Be still, and know that I am God! (Psalm 46:10)

Be still and know I am your God

Frequently in the psalms and sometimes in the prophetic books of the Old Testament, God's people were instructed to 'wait for him' or to 'wait on him'. This is the key to success as we prepare ourselves for prayer. To wait for the Lord means that we trust him and hope in him; we are putting our confidence in him and giving him priority in our lives. So we must learn to wait for him.

'Be still before the Lord, and wait patiently for him;' (Psalm 37:7);

'But those who wait for the LORD shall renew their strength, they shall mount up with wings like eagles, they shall run and not be weary, they shall walk and not faint' (Isaiah 40:31).

It is good to memorise these verses so that you have them on instant recall in your prayer time or, indeed, at any time during the day.

Whenever you have the opportunity to STOP, the verses will help you to experience the presence of Christ. Try not to let your feelings rule your life as you wait on God. Be conscious of Christ's presence, because he has promised it and his promises are unbreakable: 'Remember, I am with you always' (Matthew 28:20).

Personally, I believe it is best when emotions lie as quiet as possible. Don't try to work yourself up to a spiritual 'high', or to induce what you think is a suitable 'holy' state of mind. Allow body, mind and spirit to be as still as possible and then, during your time of prayer, if you feel that your heart is warming, thank God for it. Because you are not trying to force anything, the likely explanation is that the Holy Spirit is touching your life. Just allow the wind of the Spirit to carry you along like a sailing dinghy responding to a gentle breeze. Steer a straight course until the wind drops and the emotional period quietens — but don't forget to thank God for his special touch on your life.

Rest

This word immediately suggests to me that I should think about one of the greatest truths of the Gospel. Jesus says: 'I am the vine, you are the branches. Those who abide in me and I in them bear much fruit, because apart from me you can do nothing' (John 15:5).

Our council-built house is part of a terraced block and so it is identical to that of our neighbours. However, it does have one distinguishing feature, a flourishing grape-vine covering the back wall. Left unchecked this would spread itself in all the wrong directions; so we have trained it neatly around the windows. During the growing season we must keep pruning back the side-shoots to ensure that the fruit fully matures. It is very satisfying to see the ripening bunches of beautiful black grapes adorning the south wall of the house on late summer days. I am amazed at the strength of the parent stem which must have spread its roots deep under the house by now.

Jesus clearly loved this picture of life and growth and fruitfulness which he observed so frequently in Palestine. And in his last great I AM statement as given to us by John in his gospel, he is emphasising the need for us to abide, dwell and rest in him. He is speaking these words at the Last Supper just before his death, which gives them added importance. It would seem that he is telling us that this is the greatest secret of all Christian life — just living and remaining in him. There is no stress or strain in resting in him, there is simply the joy of his presence and the trustful quietness that it brings. If you wish to enhance the sense of his presence in your life, repeat these words slowly to yourself: 'Rest in Christ . . . dwell in him . . . Christ in me.'

As you continue using these words in an attitude of prayer, you may well find that a significant change occurs. You start this prayer affirmation by thinking of the Lord Jesus Christ as alongside but separate from you, Christ 'there' and you 'here'. The relationship is 'I : he'. But as you continue to use the prayer phrases an important change may take place. The relationship becomes more and more intimate until it is no longer 'I : he', but

'I : you'. We continue to rest in Christ, but now 'I dwell in you and you in me'.

You are resting, then, in Christ himself, and it would be natural for you to be conscious of all that he has done for you as you recall his atoning death, his risen, life-imparting presence, his actual intercession from heaven which continues until the end of time. And if your prayer were to go no further than this, you would still have reached the heart of the matter. When you have arrived at this right relationship with Jesus Christ, he is able to influence your life at every level without your necessarily having to say anything further. Probably there is much more that you want to say, but when you are resting in him and he in you, he is able to bring you guidance, strength, peace and wholeness — all radiating into you by his grace. He simply says: 'He who abides in me and I in him, the same brings forth much fruit.'

Listen

Prayer is not a monologue, it is a dialogue. If we dwell in Christ and he in us, he will wish to speak with us as much as we with him. This means that we must be open to hear his voice. How is this possible? The classic way by which he speaks to us is by our use of the Bible. Whenever we settle down for a serious prayer time, it is essential to have at least one book alongside us, and desirable to have a second. The vital book is the Bible, and it should be on hand not just for reference but for daily study. The verses will not necessarily speak to us specifically every day, although I am sure that often they will. The daily reading means that we are building up a greater knowledge of Scripture which God can use in the future.

Of course, most people need help in reading the Bible –

I know I do. Over the years I have received much help from Bible study notes produced by *The Bible Reading Fellowship, Scripture Union* and Selwyn Hughes' *Everyday with Jesus*. Since retirement I have been looking again at some of the commentaries on my bookshelf which are particularly helpful for daily Bible reading — William Barclay's *Daily Study Bible*, expositions that are still full of life; and at the moment I am looking again at William Temple's great commentary, *Readings in St John's Gospel*.

If the Bible is essential, then another book is extremely useful in my prayer time. As my mind interacts with the Holy Spirit in prayer, I find that he sometimes speaks to me through the words

A **prayer** of understanding

> It is not that conduct is all-important and prayer helps,
> but prayer is all-important and conduct tests it.
> *WILLIAM TEMPLE (1881-1944)*

of a hymn. Often, only part of a verse comes to mind, and the truth that he wants to communicate lies in the whole hymn. So if I have a hymn book to hand I can trace the full text, and the seed of thought that has come to me can be properly explored. I am sure that the Holy Spirit often uses the wealth of devotion and faith that is to be found in any hymn book to bring us encouragement, assurance and guidance.

A third book is by no means essential but some find it useful. If you have a small note-book at hand, you can write down any particularly striking thought that comes to you in your quiet time. It is also good practice to note down any important prayer requests that you make, together with the dates when you started to make them. And, of course, remember to record the dates when you are conscious that they have been answered.

All the way through this section I have been encouraging you to speak slowly and not to be afraid of repetition. I believe that it is in the quietness that the 'still small voice of God' has the best opportunity of speaking to us. Whittier's great hymn clothes this truth in beautiful language:

> Drop thy still dews of quietness,
> Till all our strivings cease:
> Take from our souls the strain and stress,
> And let our ordered lives confess
> The beauty of thy peace.
>
> Breathe through the heats of our desire
> Thy coolness and thy balm;
> Let sense be dumb, let flesh retire;
> Speak through the earthquake, wind, and fire,
> 0 still small voice of calm.

Give thanks

Someone has said that all true religion starts with grace and ends with gratitude. Grace is the totally undeserved gift of God the Father's love to us. This love was embodied in the life, death and resurrection of Jesus. And now from heaven the ascended Son interprets that love and grace to us through the work of his Holy Spirit. I am sure that the whole of our prayer life should be constantly shot through with thanksgiving. But in our human weakness we often neglect to be as grateful as we should be; so it's vital to try to ensure that thanksgiving features prominently in our prayers.

There is, perhaps, an important distinction to be made between praise and thanksgiving, although sometimes these terms are interchanged. Strictly speaking, we praise God for all that he is in his own nature, his divine being, and all that he is in

A **prayer** of confidence

> God is bound to act,
> to pour himself into thee
> as soon as he shall find thee ready.
> MEISTER ECKHART

himself. This includes, of course, praising each member of the holy Trinity for his own being and character. Thanksgiving is offered to God for all his gifts to us in creation, redemption and all the thousand parts of daily life that we so easily take for granted. 'He who gives me thanks honours me', says the psalmist, and it is good to recognise the Source of so many blessings.

When I first moved to Salisbury diocese my bishop was Joe Fison, a man who had a considerable reputation as a theologian. The first time he visited me in my parish, he asked that we should begin our time together in the church. We knelt together at the Communion rail in silent prayer. Then the bishop started to speak. I must admit that from such a scholar I was expecting a powerful theological prayer, or, at the least, one of the great Anglican collects. I was a little surprised when his first words were from a hymn:

> 'Count your blessings, name them one by one,
> And it will surprise you what the Lord has done.'

And now, some thirty-three years later, I am learning more of the secret of counting our blessings from two elderly ladies who are our next-door neighbours. Living one either side of us, and both in their eighties, they endure considerable disablement with all its attendant pain. Yet they are constantly cheerful, uncomplaining, and always ready to tell us how much they have to be thankful for! Oh for more gratitude in our prayers – and simplicity.

We started this chapter thinking about preparing for prayer. But have we noticed what has happened? The preparation has itself become prayer. James tells us to, 'Draw near to God, and he will draw near to you' (James 4:8). And so the act of will that sets in motion the practical steps of making space for God – withdrawing from activity, stilling our bodies, quietening our minds and focusing on him in a spirit of dependence and gratitude – immediately unites us with our heavenly Father. And what is prayer other than communion with him?

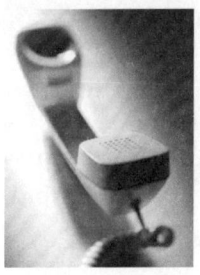

Chapter **four**

Partnership

The quality of our prayer life depends, more than anything else, on our relationship with our Lord Jesus Christ, and through him with our great Father God. Already we have seen that when we use the *abba* form of address to God we are affirming a personal relationship of profound depth. When we dwell in Christ and he dwells in us, we enjoy an intimacy in prayer that enables us to tell him everything about our lives. This is at the heart of partnership with God in prayer.

Prayer, then, is a personal conversation in which we can share everything with God, who is both the best of any parent and the truest of any friend. But because we vary in temperament, character and circumstances, we must all develop the style of conversation that suits us best and is entirely natural for us. Each of us is a unique person, whose prayer relationship with God is an individual affair.

I was once invited to take a group of church members into the local prison for an informal discussion in the chapel. The only person in our team who succeeded in communicating with the inmates was an elderly lady with a Salvation Army background.

There was nothing subtle about Vera's approach as she launched directly into her subject with enthusiasm and warmth. As the chaplain explained to us later, the men paid attention to her as to their 'mum', as she told them how special they were to God, how he cared for them individually as a father, and how every one of us is a unique creation. 'And did you know,' she said, warming to her theme, 'that no two people even have the same fingerprints?' We held our breath and groaned inwardly, but the tension was quickly broken as a voice from the back muttered, 'Yeah, we know', and everybody roared with laughter.

Yes, all so different, but all of us with the need to communicate with God in the most natural way possible. A nineteenth-century French priest, the Abbé de Tourville, wrote in his letters of direction:

> 'This is what our Lord asks of you: to be content to live with him without anxiety, without strain after perfection. Rest content with the knowledge that he in his own Person, with the Father and the Holy Spirit, is in your soul, substantially, really, literally; that he does everything you do with you, from the humblest duties to the highest. Your whole devotional life should consist in this companionship, accepted without ceremony, without intellectual or emotional effort, simply possessed and enjoyed, in perfect calmness and tranquillity. You are to say nothing to our Lord except that which comes of itself, and that in the most homely words. Never stop for a moment to ask whether or why you are worthy of this simple companionship on such a footing. Simply practise it; that is all. As for the other things, such as acts of external devotion, they are only patterns super-

imposed on that simple friendship. They should neither ruffle nor disturb its inward life.'

One of the most helpful books on prayer that has ever been published was also one of the shortest. *The Practice of the Presence of God* was written by a lay brother in a monastery. As he worked daily in the kitchen, Brother Lawrence simply trusted that Christ was with him in every mundane duty that he performed. This relationship with Jesus was such a living reality that it vitally influenced everything he did and said throughout the day. And so the specific periods set aside in the monastic life for individual or corporate prayer spilled over into all the daily activities and filled him with constant joy. What an ideal to follow!

All the way through the Bible we have examples of the natural way that different people prayed to God, each in his own individual style. Abraham is desperately concerned for members of his family who are living in the wicked city of Sodom, which is in great danger of being destroyed, owing to the evil within it. He engages in a prayer conversation with the Lord and asks whether he would destroy the city if fifty righteous people could be found in it. He deliberately pitches the number high, despite knowing it is unlikely that anything like that number will be found. When God says that he will spare the city for that number, Abraham gradually brings it down, while at the same time protesting his unworthiness: 'Let me take it upon myself to speak to the Lord, I who am but dust and ashes' (Genesis 18:27).

The full story is given in Genesis 18:22-33, and Abraham goes as far as he dares, which is to plead for ten righteous people. The relevance for us at the moment is not the outcome of his prayers but the personal and natural way that Abraham talks to God.

Or think of Hannah, the wife of Elkanah, who was desperately unhappy because she was childless. Elkanah's other wife, Peninnah, had borne him children and was constantly needling Hannah over her barrenness. Perhaps Peninnah sensed that Elkanah was especially fond of Hannah and in her jealousy was always trying to provoke her. The situation deeply disturbed Hannah, and on one occasion when the family visited the shrine at Shiloh she poured out her heart to God in prayer (1 Samuel 1:1-18). Although she was praying silently, her lips were moving in the intensity of her emotion, and Eli the priest assumed that

A **prayer** of surrender

Lord God,
I am no longer my own, but yours.
Put me to what you will,
rank me with whom you will.
Put me to doing, put me to enduring;
let me be employed for you, or laid aside for you,
exalted for you
or brought low for you;
let me be full, let me be empty;
let me have all things,
let me have nothing.
I freely and wholeheartedly yield all things
to your pleasure and disposal.
And now, glorious and blessed God,
Father, Son and Holy Spirit,
you are mine and I am yours.
So be it.
JOHN WESLEY (1703-1791)

she was drunk. Hannah countered his condemnation with, 'No, my lord, I am a woman deeply troubled; I have drunk neither wine nor strong drink, but I have been pouring out my soul before the Lord. Do not regard your servant as a worthless woman, for I have been speaking out of my great anxiety and vexation all this time' (1 Samuel 1:15, 16).

Abraham had been praying with great tact and caution, while Hannah had emotionally expressed her sorrow and frustration with tears and passionate words that were entirely natural to her.

There was never a more reluctant prophet than Jeremiah. He was a shy man with a sensitive nature, yet God gave him one of the hardest messages for any prophet to proclaim. He constantly went back to the Lord to draw strength from him through prayer. Listen to his very personal cry when the task seemed totally beyond him: 'O Lord, you have enticed me, and I was enticed; you have overpowered me, and you have prevailed. I have become a laughingstock all day long; everyone mocks me. For whenever I speak, I must cry out, I must shout, "Violence and destruction!" For the word of the Lord has become for me a reproach and derision all day long. If I say, "I will not mention him, or speak any more in his name," then within me there is something like a burning fire shut up in my bones; I am weary with holding it in, and I cannot' (Jeremiah 20:7-9).

This prayer of Jeremiah shows the intensity of the inner struggle with his vocation. The vital characteristic is that he is releasing his problem onto the Lord and telling him exactly how he is feeling.

Daniel was a man of prayer who was deeply disciplined and never missed those times during the day he had determined to give to God: 'He continued to go to his house, which had windows in its upper room open towards Jerusalem, and to get down on his knees three times a day to pray to his God and praise him, just as he had done previously' (Daniel 6:10). Nothing, it seemed, could deflect Daniel from his habitual prayer, not even the threat of death!

There was quiet, concentrated practice about Daniel's prayer life which was totally personal as he praised God for his grace and sought his mercy each day. Being a Jew, it is likely that he sometimes prayed in a formal and liturgical manner, but we can see from Daniel's life of faith that his prayers would certainly have been spoken with sincerity and spiritual warmth.

The disciplined order of Daniel's prayer life is an inspiration to us all. Because of our differing personalities and spiritual backgrounds, some of us will be happier with a more formal and structured prayer partnership with God. The importance lies in the depth of the relationship, rather than the formality or informality of the words we use.

Once again, the greatest example is found in the prayer experience of Jesus. A number of gospel passages show Jesus praying at special times of need or at turning points in his life and ministry. For instance, his forty days in the desert following his baptism in the Holy Spirit. It has been suggested that when he went into the desert he did not know whether he should be a welfare Messiah, one who would win people over by force, or whether he should try to influence them by performing dramatic and supernatural feats. If that suggestion carries weight, through prayer and meditation on the Scriptures he would have come to see each of those roads as a cul-de-sac, and that he was called to become a suffering Messiah.

On another occasion, as his mission gathered momentum, he

realised that he needed to train twelve men as the leaders of the New Israel. So he set aside a whole night for prayer to decide who should be singled out from the many followers who had been attracted to him. Luke records that all-night prayer vigil (Luke 6:12-16).

A **prayer** of receptivity

> A revised version of your life is published
> every time you pray, really pray.
> For in the silence before him,
> You bring more and more areas of your life under his control,
> more and more powers are put at his disposal,
> more and more channels of receptivity are opened up
> and more and more alignments of our wills
> are made to the will of God.
> TOYOHIKO KAGAWA (1888-1960)

Again Luke reports that Jesus was praying on the Mount of Transfiguration as he prepared himself for the final phase of his ministry, which would reach its climax in his crucifixion (Luke 9:28-32).

All these prayer experiences were at times of crises for Jesus, but every day his partnership in prayer with his Father lay at the heart of all that he did and said during every hour of his ministry. In particular, John's gospel reveals how Jesus' prayer meditation keeps breaking through in his life. Most notably this is seen in the account of Jesus at the Last Supper. The heart of his prayer at the end of the meal is an intercession for his friends who are sitting round the table with him, that they may be guided, empowered, and remain in unity with one another and with him. It concludes with a similar prayer for all those who will believe in him through their witness; so we, too, are included. But the prayer begins with sublime words which show the perfect prayer partnership between Father and Son:

> 'Father, the hour has come; glorify your Son so that the Son may glorify you, since you have given him authority over all people, to give eternal life to all whom you have given him. And this is eternal life, that they may know you, the only true God, and Jesus Christ whom you have sent. I have glorified you on earth by finishing the work that you gave me to do. So now, Father, glorify me in your own presence with the glory that I had in your presence before the world existed'
> (John 17:1-5).

Jesus' prayers were so natural with his Father: whatever was on his mind he expressed. Perhaps the nearest human picture we can find is the marriage relationship at its best. Here, two people are in perfect unity and harmony together and able to share all that they are thinking and feeling with each other in the most natural language. In fact, they will not be thinking about the words at all; they just talk; words simply flow. Joys and problems are shared; requests made; and sometimes fears and anxieties are expressed. At other times disagreements have to be aired, grievances admitted, perhaps forcibly and emotionally. We have good biblical precedence for that kind of prayer as we have just seen in Jeremiah, and will see shortly in David's prayer life as revealed to us in the Psalms.

For Jesus, prayer was more than an exercise, it was a partnership. As with marriage, or any deep relationship, the lines of communication have to be kept open. So Jesus felt the need to pray frequently. And if he needed to, how much more do we.

Chapter **five**

Problems

Let us now consider some of the problems which can crop up in our praying. Hopefully, this will turn out to be a positive exercise, because in considering the answers to such difficulties we shall be restating some of the most profound principles of prayer.

A problem which is frequently raised is a serious one and must be faced right at the beginning. It poses the question: if God is almighty and all-knowing and foresees everything that is going to happen, what is the point of praying? We surely can't change his divine will. Therefore, the best course is to leave everything to his wisdom and allow him to work things out in his way. In other words, just accept what comes because his omnipotence is sovereign.

I know of some mature Christians who pray regularly, truly commune with God and make acts of adoration, confession and thanksgiving; but they only rarely make a prayer request because of this theological difficulty.

Yet we know that both the Old and New Testaments of the Bible contain many examples of petition and intercession and, what is more, they clearly encourage us to use such forms of prayer ourselves. Take, for instance, Jesus' instruction: 'Ask, and it will be given to you; search, and you will find; knock, and the door will be opened for you' (Luke 11:9). And the prayer that Jesus specially taught us to use has six separate acts of petition, making up at least three quarters of the prayer. So how can we resolve this conflict?

First, when the biblical evidence is so strong, we must suspect that there is something wrong with our human reasoning if we decide to ignore it. The second point is simple but fundamental. Yes, God the almighty One does indeed know all things, but the greatest revelation that Jesus gave us is that he is our heavenly Father. This is the beginning of all prayer: 'When you pray, say: "Father . . ."' (Luke 11:2).

Everything that is perfect in fatherhood is revealed in God, and every good father wants the best for his children. he understands their needs and he desires to give good gifts to them at the best possible time and in the best possible situation. he knows that their wants and requests are not always beneficial for them in the long term, let alone the present. He perfectly understands if the timing is right for these good gifts. Both perfect wisdom and divine love meet at this point. A mature human father does not resent his children's asking for anything that is good in itself. He will normally welcome the request, because it shows that the child has reached the point where he or she will truly appreciate the granting of the request and understand its significance. Then finally, when the positive answer comes, there will be true gratitude. And if the answer is negative then the relationship is such that the father is still trusted about the situation.

Some of our prayer requests are complex. They may sound

simple to us; we just want a 'yes' or a 'no' — more often the former. But our heavenly Father sees the involvement of a whole web of complicated circumstances which will have to be changed, unravelled or re-ordered before the seemingly simple answer can be given. But surely, although he knows all things, our Father wants us to ask him so that we can trust him with our deepest as well as our ordinary needs. The asking signifies that we will know the true Source of the answer when it comes. In this way our faith in him and love for him are strengthened.

A **prayer** of appreciation

> Forgive me, Lord,
> for a mind that turns so readily to weigh my troubles,
> so seldom to count my blessings.
> Teach me the practice of recollection,
> the habit of thankfulness,
> and the art of praise.
> And may I deal as generously with others as you deal with me.
>
> T. DUDLEY-SMITH

Here is one of the most significant statements about prayer that I have ever come across, made by Archbishop Trench when he said, 'Prayer is not overcoming God's reluctance, it is laying hold of his highest willingness.' And Jesus himself laid down the principle: 'If you then, who are evil, know how to give good gifts to your children, how much more will your Father in Heaven give good things to those who ask him!' (Matthew 7:11).

The next problem I want to consider is much more practical, and concerns the tendency of most of us when we pray to allow our thoughts to wander. We should not become too uptight about this, because our minds have been programmed to work in thought sequences. So, for most people, wandering thoughts are inevitable. If we pray for Auntie Flo who is having an operation next week, our minds will probably flick from her present prob-

A **prayer** of usefulness

> Lord Jesus Christ,
> Master Carpenter of Nazareth,
> who through wood and nails has wrought our full salvation,
> wield well thy tools in this thy workshop,
> that we, who come to thee rough hewn,
> may be fashioned to a truer usefulness and beauty by thy hand,
> and thine be the glory always.
>
> (ANON)

lems to the moment when we last saw her eighteen months ago on our west country holiday. And then a series of pleasant pictures will chase across the screen of our minds as we recall the highlights of the holiday. But this year's holiday will be in Wales and we must visit that amazing waterfall that we read about in the guide book last week; and there's Cader Idris to climb, if it's not quite beyond us at our age. Oh dear! Poor Auntie Flo seems to have disappeared from view; and Christopher Robin, it seems, is not in a class of his own when it comes to praying.

There are two pieces of advice which may possibly help us with this problem, although I doubt if we shall ever eliminate it.

First, it is so important to still the mind. A quiet mind will tend to stay focused on God and the true needs that we want to bring to him. If we practise the presence of God, our minds will gradually become still before him. It is a great help to repeat scriptural words that encourage us into an experience of God's peace, such as:

'Be still, and know that I am God!' (Psalm 46:10)

'Be still before the Lord, and wait patiently for him;' (Psalm 37:7)

'For God alone my soul waits in silence.' (Psalm 62:1)

'Peace I leave with you; my peace I give to you.' (John 14:27)

God's word has a unique authority, and it will often have a deeply calming effect on our minds and so aid us in concentration.

Secondly, we can overcome distracting thoughts by making our imaginations work for us in a more creative way. The simplest way to do this is to have a picture of Jesus in our minds. Perhaps we have been struck by a great painting of him and can now recall his features. Or we can build up our own picture of him. Or again, we might use the technique employed in the film *Ben Hur*, in which the face of Jesus is never shown but his presence is powerfully sensed by the falling of a shadow, a pair of outstretched hands, or by a distant back view of him teaching on the mountainside. In whichever way is most helpful for us, we should bring our friends into his presence, picture them kneeling before him, sense his concern for them, and know that his power flows into them as he touches them. Picture Jesus standing or seated, as seems more appropriate, and introduce to him all who need his help. Hold them, one by one, peacefully in his presence for a few moments. Trust him to know their problems and deepest needs and be conscious of his compassion and grace filling them.

Another very common prayer problem is to know what to do when our emotions are discordant and uncontrollable. Sometimes sitting down in quietness makes us feel worse. We know that we ought to pray but our inward feelings are pulling us apart. Often we have to admit that we don't really know what is happening. At other times we can identify a sense of stress, anxiety, fear or depression, but giving a name to the inward condition doesn't cure it.

A **prayer** of waiting

> O Lord, I do not know what to ask of you.
> You alone know my true needs.
> You love me more than I myself know how to love.
> Help me to see my real needs which are concealed from me.
> I dare not ask either a cross or a consolation.
> I can only wait upon you.
> My heart is open to you.
> Visit and help me, for your great mercy's sake.
> (FROM THE RUSSIAN ORTHODOX LITURGY)

We should begin by reminding ourselves that we pray by faith and not by feeling. The very fact that our feelings are working against us shows that faith is the only answer. When we speak of faith we mean the medium by which we make contact with God. We don't have faith in faith, but rather *by* faith we affirm and trust the real and living presence of the Lord. And in this matter the great promises of Scripture are special aids to faith.

So in these difficult periods when you seem least capable of prayer, remember the words of the medieval German mystic, Johannes 'Meister' Eckhart: 'God is bound to act, to pour himself into thee, as soon as he shall see thee ready.' Simply start by telling the Lord that you want to pray, that you are willing to pray, that you can't pray today with any feeling of warmth, joy, love or thankfulness, but that you will try to pray with your will alone. And if you can't even do this, then perhaps you can at least pray, 'Lord, I am willing to be made willing.' Be encouraged, for this is one of the most profound prayers that you can ever make.

It is when we feel weakest and most vulnerable that the promises of God can make their deepest impact. For as we hold them in our minds we are affirming that, beyond our sense of failure, God is trustworthy, and that he can never ever allow one of his promises to fail. We, being human, sadly break our promises from time to time, but God can never do this.

I suggest, then, that you take the promise which the Lord gave Paul when he was most conscious of weakness and bewilderment in his own life: 'My grace is sufficient for you, for power is made perfect in weakness' (2 Corinthians 12:9).

Lay hold of God's highest willingness to help you. Picture that promise as given to yourself, repeat the words slowly, allowing them to sink deeply into your mind. God knows all about your situation. One of the greatest prayers in the Anglican prayer book begins, 'Almighty God, to whom all hearts are open, all desires known and from whom no secrets are hidden . . . .' (*The Alternative Service Book*). As Paul discovered, it is when we are at our weakest, and fully aware of it, that God can help us most.

When that promise has really sunk in, then move on to others, such as: 'Humble yourselves therefore under the mighty hand of God, so that he may exalt you in due time. Cast all your anxiety on him, because he cares for you' (1 Peter 5:6, 7) or 'My God will fully satisfy every need of yours according to his riches in glory in Christ Jesus' (Philippians 4:19).

Prayer based on the promises of God is always powerful because it is grounded on faith, not feelings. However, that does not mean that we should never experience love and joy in prayer. In fact, because we vary in temperament and disposition, some of us at least will experience great love and joy welling up within ourselves as we pray. But the really vital factor is the depth of our relationship, rather than the extravagance of our feelings. As I have already suggested, if we begin our prayers in the quietness of the presence of Christ, the Holy Spirit will lift us to a true emotional level that is natural for us. In the quietness we should allow the dew of God's Spirit to refresh us. May these words quoted by Kathryn Kuhn, a missionary in Burma, speak to us:

> 'Quietness and absorption bring the dew. At night, when the leaf and blade are still, the vegetable pores are open to receive the refreshing and invigorating bath; so spiritual dew comes from the quiet lingering in the Master's presence. Get still before him. Haste will prevent you receiving the dew. Wait before God until you feel saturated with his presence . . . . Dew will never gather while there is heat or wind; so the peace of God

does not come forth to rest the soul until the STILL point is reached.'

If a spirit of heaviness and dullness persists, we should try concentrating on one form of prayer alone – thanksgiving. We can look around us, look back, and focus on every detail of our lives that can be turned into thanksgiving. We can oserve the world of nature, recognise the value of friendships, look through the familiar into the depth of family life and the daily blessings that are so easily taken for granted. Even watching television can help us to realise how rich we are in our possessions as we see that millions of others are denied even the basic necessities of life such as food, clothing, shelter, freedom. Occasionally, a heart-warming incident will stand out amid so much depressing news, as when the *Daily Mail* published the prayer of a teenaged girl written shortly before her death from cancer:

'Thanks, God, for listening to me all those times I wanted to talk to you. Even though I go on a bit. Thanks for helping me when I asked. And thanks for laughter. Thank you God, for Michael Jackson, loud music, ballet and snow flakes . . . . And when it's time to put away all the things you gave me, please God don't let me say why? Let me say, Thanks!'

Yes, we cannot find it difficult to be truly thankful, given an example like this to inspire us.

Above all, look up and take a fresh look at Jesus, who he is and what he has done for you. Focus again on the love of God, and thank him.

You may have noticed how often I have advocated repetition in prayer, and this may have raised a problem for some of you. It is true that Jesus himself warned against the danger of vain, mindless repetition in prayer, which monotonously repeats some concerns that we have, with the assumption that the more we engage in such rituals the more likely God is to answer. Jesus said that the Pharisees were prone to this problem, which implied that they believed constant repetition would somehow bend God's ear.

However, from what we have already discovered I hope it is obvious that this attitude is the absolute opposite of what God, the Father of our Lord Jesus Christ, is really like. He is the God of all grace, the perfect 'abba' heavenly Father, whose highest willingness is to give gifts to his children. The only reason that I have emphasised the place of repetition in prayer is for *our* sakes, not God's! We need it because of our human weakness when we are engaged in this highest of spiritual activities. Michael Ramsey has given wise words on this matter:

> '. . . repetition, many times and many times, is found to quieten the distracting parts of our personalities and to keep us wonderfully subdued and concentrated, and as we repeat the words again and again we bring into our hearts the many people and needs about whom we really want to pray. As the words proceed, the heart has the people on it one by one.'

This is exceptionally sound advice. Let me illustrate it. Go back to Philippians 4:19 which we looked at earlier, and as you mentally repeat the words of this verse, breathe deeply and allow them to line up with your breathing rhythm.

> My . . . God . . . supplies
> All . . . your . . . needs
> Through his glorious . . . riches
> In . . . Christ . . . Jesus

Quietly repeat these words for several minutes as you realise their significance for your own situation at the present moment. Be assured that the Lord knows all about it. Slowly revolve the words around your mind so that they begin to influence you at a deep level. Trust them, rejoice in them. Realise afresh all the divine resources that are available as Jesus Christ himself engages in heavenly intercession for you (Romans 8:34; Hebrews 7:25). Remember that he wants you to cast all your care on him because he cares so much for you. Allow these words to influence every part of your life and know that the Lord is able to control your circumstances.

But this is not all. As you quietly repeat these words, move outwards from your own situation, and think of members of your family and your friends and neighbours who have special needs, and bring them into your prayer. Say the prayer of affirmation from Philippians 4:19 with them in mind. Superimpose it, as it were, over their life situations. If you find it helpful, use again the mental picture of Jesus laying hands on them. In doing this you are radiating God's life and love into them, and releasing all the resources of the Holy Spirit into their being.

This is very far from 'vain repetition'. It is taking the reality of God's grace and applying it, by faith, to the whole of our lives and to the lives of those for whom we pray. It is allowing the Holy Spirit to release life-changing influences at the deepest point of need.

We have been looking at problems which arise in prayer owing to an intellectual, emotional or spiritual difficulty. Ultimately these are our own problems; they are within our own minds and can cause considerable distress. As we conclude this chapter, I want to leave you with one overriding thought.

On the day of resurrection, according to John's gospel, the disciples were together in a room where the doors had been locked for fear of the Jews: 'Then Jesus came and stood among them and said, "Peace be with you".' Sometimes we ourselves live in a 'locked room'. The lock is on the inside because of some neg-

A **prayer** for goodness

> O Holy Spirit, giver of light and life;
> Impart to us thoughts higher than our own thoughts,
> prayers better than our own prayers,
> and powers beyond our own powers;
> That we may spend and be spent in the ways of love and goodness,
> after the perfect image of our Lord and Saviour, Jesus Christ.
>
> E. MILNER-WHITE

ative reaction that we have made either to life or to God. Sometimes it will be fear, but there may be some other negative source. Let's remember that Jesus Christ is not limited by our problems. As the risen Lord, he is able to pass through locked doors. When prayer becomes difficult I sometimes use these prayer fragments:

> Doors being shut
> Then came Jesus
> 'Peace, be still'

However bad I feel, however firmly bolted the door, the risen Lord always responds to the prayer: 'Lord, I am willing to be made willing'.

Chapter **six**

Peace

Isaiah made a promise in the name of God about those who centre their lives on the Lord: 'You will keep in perfect peace him whose mind is steadfast, because he trusts in you' (Isaiah 26:3, NIV).

Paul personalises this promise to his friends at Philippi when he affirms that: 'the peace of God, which surpasses all understanding, will guard your hearts and your minds in Christ Jesus' (Philippians 4:7).

If we go back to the Hebrew which lies behind the English word, we find one of the richest words in the human language. 'Shalom' is rightly translated as 'peace', but the Hebrew word implies more than peace: peace in all its fulness in every dimension of existence, peace of mind, peace in relationships, harmony and integration of emotions and spirit and an overall sense of peace and wellbeing in one's life. And, most fundamentally, peace *with* God which gradually radiates into all aspects of life as the peace *of* God.

We have peace with God through the atoning death of his Son Jesus Christ. Paul makes this absolutely clear in his greatest letter when he writes: 'Now that we have been put right with God through faith, we have peace with God through our Lord Jesus Christ. He has brought us by faith into this experience of God's grace, in which we now live' (Romans 5:1, 2, TEV).

And so we have only to make our response to God's initiative — his reaching out to us in love and grace through his Son — to have peace with him and consequently to experience his peace in our lives. This is beautifully illustrated in Jesus' story of the prodigal son. The young tearaway returned home hoping to make peace with his father, only to find that his father had already made peace with him: 'This son of mine' (Luke 15:24). No wonder they celebrated!

The father's kiss and embrace and his gifts of the new clothes, the ring, the shoes and the party were sacramental signs that the relationship was re-established, that reconciliation was complete and his unconditional acceptance a reality. Then when the party was over, it was back to normal life, the everyday routine of work and play, of living together in the family, and all the while being filled with a sense of wellbeing as he enjoyed the security of his father's love.

Peace with God starts at the deepest centre of our being. The Hebrews thought of that as being the heart, but it means much more than merely the emotional dimension of life. In fact, it involves our total consciousness, not just feelings but the operation of the mind and human will as well. This profound reconciliation with God that Jesus Christ has effected means that, once God's peace has become established in our hearts through faith in Christ's atoning victory, we can move on to discover more and more of the actual peace of God in our lives. Part of our understanding of that victory is to be able to affirm that Jesus Christ is bigger than any problem which we face in life which threatens our peace of mind.

In human terms, there could be no ending to the horrors of World War II until a decisive victory had taken place. Only then could peace start to become a reality, although there were many

> ### A **prayer** of guidance
>
> O Lord God,
> I thank you for the growing knowledge of myself,
> of the depths of personality which affect my thinking,
> my feeling, my behaviour and my dreams.
> There is much more than I ever thought,
> so much more to offer to you,
> for the cleansing and sanctifying of your Spirit.
> Heal my inner divisions in the unity of your will;
> set my fears at rest in your love and grace;
> let no resentments destroy my inner peace,
> no thoughts of self deflect me from your purpose for me.
> Help me to grow towards the fulness of life and love
> seen in your blessed Son, Jesus Christ, my Lord.
>
> *GEORGE APPLETON*

difficult years before the full fruits of peace were enjoyed. Once peace with God through Christ has become true for us, then the peace of God starts to influence every aspect of our lives. This peace will begin to bring a quiet, strong sense of direction to our wills, a warm stability to our emotions and a fresh clarity to our minds. This new integration of personality enables the love of

God to rise up in our hearts and then to be radiated outwards to others. This harmonisation deep within our inner lives is the secret of joy.

All true prayer will usually lead to a sense of God's grace in our lives. Sometimes it may bring other experiences such as joy and inner strength. But the most natural prayer experience is a sense of the peace of God. I don't think that it is helpful to set out deliberately to stir up our emotions in prayer, but rather the first movement should be a resting in Christ. Any emotions which then arise during prayer will probably be the work of the Holy Spirit. Apart from other important reasons, this is a vital consideration in starting each day in prayer. When we do this we create the conditions in which God's peace can rule our hearts during the day, whatever stresses or strains we may be subjected to.

The more we pray, the more we are likely to find a growing sense of assurance of faith developing within us. Frequently people can be heard expressing longings for more faith in Christ: 'I like to think that I trust him' they say; or 'How I wish I could be more certain'; or 'If only I could be sure'. The answer lies in trusting the promises of God and then praying them. 'Anyone who comes to me I will never drive away' (John 6:37) is a definitive promise of Jesus Christ. In times of doubt and uncertainty, remind him of it in prayer. Of course, we know our Lord does not need any reminding, those words are engraved on his heart, as it were. But he loves to hear us reminding ourselves of the rock-like eternity of his promises when we pray. It shows him that we mean business, and that our faith is not based on shallow emotionalism but on the foundation of the word of God.

It follows from this that all prayer has a healing quality, as the different parts of life, which can be so discordant, are brought together in harmony and unity. But the peace of prayer can also be specifically focused for particular healing needs in the realms of body and mind, as well as spirit.

In Mark 2:1-12 Jesus is presented with a difficult case of illness. The scene unfolds in near farce. Following his initial teaching-healing tour of the hinterland of Galilee, he has now returned to home-base at Capernaum. Mark records that Jesus is 'at home', which presumably means the house of one of his close disciples, perhaps Peter. His return is immediately spotted, and the house is surrounded by local people who want to hear more of his fascinating stories and to bring their friends for his healing touch. The incident involves a man who has a major problem of paralysis and so is unable to approach near enough to beg for healing. Fortunately, he has four friends who are happy to carry his stretcher, but they find that the crowd has blocked the way to Jesus. Being a determined group, they seize on a possible way out of the problem. The typical Palestinian house would have had access to a flat roof, and the four friends simply haul up the stretcher so that it is placed above the room where Jesus is teaching. But there is still a solid ceiling of plaster and lathe between him and them.

The crowd underneath probably first hear strange scraping noises and the odd thump coming from above. Then bits of plaster begin to fall on their heads, followed by pieces of broken wood until, finally, looking up they see the sky above them. At this point I'm surprised that the whole ceiling didn't collapse with all five men plus stretcher ending up in a heap on the floor below! Fortunately, the house is well built; the roof holds; and the stretcher is carefully lowered right to the feet of Jesus.

The commotion and the comedy are over, and Jesus takes control of the situation. With his spiritual gift of discernment he looks deep into the paralysed man's mind and senses the source of his problem. He sees that behind his physical paralysis lies spiritual dis-ease. Something had gone wrong in this man's past life, and the inter-relationship between body, mind and spirit is so strong that the deep-seated inward malaise has now manifested in an outward physical problem. Jesus goes straight to the heart of the matter when he pronounces, 'Son, your sins are forgiven' (Mark 2:5).

There are other important factors in this incident. Jesus discerns the hostile reaction of the Jewish scribes who are present. They have been quick to see the implication of Jesus' words and start muttering among themselves that only God can forgive sins; so who on earth does this young upstart rabbi think he is? Jesus answers their criticism by giving proof of his authority by linking the inner forgiveness with the outward healing of this needy man. The spiritual healing is confirmed as the man picks up his stretcher and walks gratefully home.

Another significant factor is the statement that Jesus was able to act because he saw 'their faith'. Clearly, the four men trusted that Jesus could help their friend, who himself might well have believed that Jesus could do something for him, while yet being unaware of his deep-seated problem.

This, then, is one of Jesus' most interesting and significant healing miracles, not only for the very human details it gives us, but also because it shows us that Jesus is able to penetrate to the problem behind the problem. He understood every facet of the situation and discerned the full dimension of the man's need and so could bring total healing.

The paralysed man went home at peace with God because he had received the divine, authoritative word of forgiveness from Jesus himself. The peace of God was a reality to him then because God had proved to be greater than his problem. Of course, he would need to keep closely in tune with God's new life within him. It would need to be nourished and renewed, but that new life had begun.

A **prayer** of thanks

Christ was all anguish that I might be all joy,
cast off that I might be brought in,
trodden down as an enemy
that I might be welcomed as a friend,
surrendered to hell's worst
that I might attain heaven's best,
stripped that I might be clothed,
wounded that I might be healed,
athirst that I might drink,
tormented that I might be comforted,
made a shame that I might inherit glory,
entered darkness that I might have eternal light.
My saviour wept that all tears might be wiped from my eyes,
groaned that I might have endless song,
endured all pain that I might have unfading health,
bore a thorned crown that I might have a glory diadem,
bowed his head that I might uplift mine,
experienced reproach that I might receive welcome,
closed his eyes in death that I might gaze on unclouded brightness,
expired that I might for ever live.

ATTRIBUTED TO RICHARD BAXTER (1615-1691)

As we pray that the peace of God may be constantly renewed in our hearts, there are a number of ways in which we may experience this inner healing. Try using short scriptural sentences that have a specific reference to wholeness, and think of the biblical truth that lies behind them.

During his three-year earthly ministry, Jesus was both a teacher and a healer; his healing ministry was integral to his saving plan. But Jesus is now ascended to the right hand of his Father, and he has taken up into heaven with him all that he was on earth. And because he is 'the same yesterday and today and forever' (Hebrews 13:8), we know that his healing ministry continues today through his Holy Spirit who is his personal – active – presence on earth. We can picture, then, his healing and life-giving power still flowing from heaven into people's lives on earth, wherever he finds a situation of 'seeing their faith . . . '.

As we sit quietly in prayer, opening up to God and welcoming Christ's healing touch, we can picture God speaking to us in words such as: 'I am the Lord who heals you' (Exodus 15:26). It's often helpful to repeat the words silently in our minds. Just be still — the shalom of God is at work.

Another Old Testament prayer sentence that can be used for healing and wholeness comes from the great suffering servant vision of Isaiah: 'By his wounds we are healed' (Isaiah 53:5, NIV).

At one point in his gospel, Matthew tries to sum up Jesus' healing ministry with an appropriate Old Testament quotation and he finds what he wants in Isaiah 53:

> 'When evening came, people brought to Jesus many who had demons in them. Jesus drove out the evil spirits with a word and healed all who were sick. He did

this to make what the prophet Isaiah had said come true. "He himself took our sicknesses and carried away our diseases." ' (Matthew 8:16, 17, GNB.)

Although Matthew quotes Isaiah 53:4, we can use verse five, 'By his wounds we are healed', to show how he is interpreting the healing ministry of Jesus in terms of the cross where he won the final victory over sin, disease, evil and suffering.

Again, repeat these six words really slowly and allow your

A **prayer** for holiness

> Teach me, O God,
> so to use all the circumstances of my life today
> that they may bring forth in me the fruits of holiness
> rather than the fruits of sin.
> Let me use disappointments as material for patience:
> Let me use success as material for thankfulness:
> Let me use suspense as material for perseverance:
> Let me use danger as material for courage:
> Let me use reproach as material for longsuffering:
> Let me use praise as material for humility:
> Let me use pleasure as material for temperance:
> Let me use pains as material for endurance.
>
> *J. N. BAILLIE (1886-1960)*

breathing to deepen as you say them. You will be releasing healing powers into your mind, and from there into your emotions and body. Surely there is an eternal stream of divine healing love radiating day and night from Christ's cross, and by using these words you are simply focusing that spiritual healing power into your life, and into that of your family and friends. You are affirming that Jesus Christ's healing power is radiating into the lives of all those you bring to God in prayer: 'I am the Lord who heals you' . . . *because* 'By my wounds you are healed.' I don't think that it distorts the meaning of those last six words if you change them slightly. By using a different pronoun you move the emphasis from what Christ says to you to what you affirm to him in response: 'By *your* wounds we are healed'.

The truth embraces both statements and so they are equally valid as we engage in prayer for healing and wholeness.

Another helpful healing prayer is based on Jesus' great saying, 'I am the Light of the world.' Light has healing qualities, and the mental picture of Jesus shining the light of his Spirit within us is a life-giving one. Imagine the Lord saying to you: 'I am the Light of the world within you; your life is filled with light.'

As we use the words, repeating them quietly to ourselves, God's light is driving out the darkness that is within us all because, sadly, there is always some aspect in us of darkness whether sin, ignorance or dis-ease.

Staying with the reality of God as light for a little longer, take this prayer sentence: 'I am sunbathing in God's healing light'.

Picture yourself at rest, perfectly still, just luxuriating in the rays of God's healing light and love as they shine over you and into you. Use this imaginative picture for your friends as well. Hold them in these glorious life-giving rays of divine light. Christ's light is shining into every part of their lives — body, mind, bloodstream, even nerve fibres — penetrating deeply into every crevice, even to the subconscious mind.

As we conclude our thinking about the peace of prayer, let's go back finally to the cross. We've had open Bibles, and now we turn to our hymnbook, and Bishop Walsham How's moving lines:

> 0 my Saviour lifted
> From the earth for me,
> Draw me in thy mercy,
> Nearer unto thee.
>
> Lift my earthbound longings,
> Fix them, Lord, above;
> Draw me with the magnet
> Of thy mighty love.
>
> And I come, Lord Jesus;
> Dare I turn away?
> No! Thy love hath conquered,
> And I come today;
>
> Bringing all my burdens,
> Sorrow, sin and care,
> At thy feet I lay them,
> And I leave them there.

The first two verses are a prayer, while the last two are an affirmation and response flowing out from that prayer. Because of Christ's conquering love we can bring all our burdens to the cross. And what are they? Sin is anything which spoils our relationship with God or other people; sorrow is deep sadness – hurts, disappointments, regret, bereavement and loss, and suchlike. And care, I suggest, is anything that weighs us down –

anxiety, stress, insecurity, doubts and fears, anything that robs us of our peace of mind.

Remembering what Jesus Christ has done for us on his cross, seeing afresh the revelation of divine love at Calvary, we come back to our Lord Jesus Christ, bringing with us everything that spoils our life in the present moment and which tends to destroy our peace. We now quite deliberately and purposefully lay all these burdens at the foot of his cross and we walk away, having left them once and for all, where Jesus has dealt with them. And the result? 'Those of steadfast mind you keep in peace – in peace because they trust in you' (Isaiah 26:3).

Chapter **seven**

Penitence

It is a remarkable fact that two of the greatest men of God in the Bible are also, to outward appearances, two of the greatest sinners.

David was, by far, the most important king in Israel's history. Apart from Moses, no other person had such a powerful and lasting influence on Jewish national life, or was more effective in building a powerful and secure kingdom. No other man in the pages of the Old Testament has revealed so much of his inner life as has David in his many psalms. David's poems give us a window into his emotional and spiritual experiences and we will look more closely at some of these in a later chapter. We cannot but be moved as we see beneath the surface into the inner depths of his mind through these illuminating psalms. We can view his fear, depression, paranoia and blazing anger, as well as his joy, exultation, euphoria, sense of peace and – at times – overflowing love.

In his day, David was a man whom most respected and many loved. He had been enthusiastically accepted as the head of a new royal dynasty by his fellow countrymen, excepting only the family and friends of the former king, Saul. But there came a point in the noonday of his success when he was irresistibly attracted to a married woman. He not only seduced her, making her pregnant, but by means of a despicable underhand plot he contracted the death of her husband. He, the King, the source of final authority and justice in the land, manipulated events to his own utterly selfish ends. David, the great hero, the father of his people, the conqueror of the Philistines, the saviour of his nation, the holy man of faith who had trusted in the living God so deeply through all his years of danger and exile, was a flagrant sinner.

The whole squalid episode is recorded in 2 Samuel 11:2-17.

One of the most surprising aspects of the event was that David wasn't particularly troubled by it. There is nothing to suggest that, at the time, he suffered any qualms of conscience or had any inner questionings about what he had done. So it was that, months later, God sent the prophet Nathan to David to confront him with his great moral failure by means of a simple parable.

Nathan must have entered the King's presence with considerable apprehension. In our contemporary constitutional understanding we would regard David as a dictator; certainly he was an absolute monarch. He was also a highly emotional man, as his psalms reveal. David's reaction to the truth that Nathan had to uncover was quite unpredictable. The prophet's parable opened up the subject of guilt in an oblique way and initially evoked David's sympathy for the victim and anger against the perpetrator of such a heinous crime. Then came the crunch as Nathan addressed David in just four words: 'You are the man'.

How would the King react? Would there be a volcanic explosion of anger at the sheer effrontery of addressing the King's majesty in such words? Would Nathan be led off, never to be seen again? Would his whole family be liquidated?

No, the devastating words struck home because there was supernatural power and authority behind them. Nathan was simply giving the message that had first come from the Lord himself. The blockage in David's spiritual perception was penetrated and the truth about what he had done was exposed. To his credit, he immediately confessed his guilt: 'I have sinned against the Lord' (2 Samuel 12:1-15). David asked for and received forgiveness, but the consequences of this spiritual disaster can be

A **prayer** for forgiveness

Forgive them all, O Lord:
our sins of omission and our sins of commission;
the sins of our youth and the sins of our bodies;
our secret and our more open sins;
our sins of ignorance and surprise,
and our more deliberate and presumptuous sins;
the sins we have done to please others;
the sins we know and remember,
and the sins we have forgotten;
the sins we have striven to hide from others
and the sins by which we have made others offend;
forgive them, O Lord,
forgive them all for his sake,
who died for our sins and rose for our justification,
and now stands at thy right hand to make intercession for us,
Jesus Christ our Lord.
JOHN WESLEY (1703-1791)

detected in later parts of his life. God continued to guide him, and his reign proceeded to the final honoured conclusion, but his moral authority was never the same again.

But even David never went as far astray as the apostle Paul. The man who is responsible for almost half of the New Testament and who is the greatest theologian that the Christian church has ever known is the same man who made a claim for himself that David never dreamt of. In this one uncompromising statement, he reveals the truth about his inner life: 'Here is a trustworthy saying that deserves full acceptance: Christ Jesus came into the world to save sinners – *of whom I am the worst*" (1 Timothy 1:15, NIV, my italics).

Paul is writing to his young friend and colleague, Timothy, towards the end of his own life. Probably Paul is under house arrest in Rome and almost all his great missionary achievements are behind him. Of course, he knows he is a forgiven sinner; all his preaching gives evidence of that, but he can never forget his past. He still recalls those days when as chief of the Sanhedrin secret police he arrested and imprisoned many of the first Christians, some of whom were subsequently executed. Above all, he still lives with the memory of his part as ringleader in the death of the young charismatic Christian leader, Stephen. He can never forget that horrific episode when, although he had not thrown a single rock, he had been the instigator of Stephen's ritual murder.

We know that Stephen's death came back to haunt Paul because he refered to it years later when he himself narrowly escaped being lynched. He was rescued from the Jerusalem mob by the local Roman guard and allowed to make a defence before the people. In the course of this defence he refers to a previous visit to Jerusalem following his conversion to Christ. At that moment, he says, he was reliving the details of Stephen's death (Acts 22:17-20). And so all the way through his life Paul felt that no one could ever sink lower than he had.

As we can see from the Bible, sin is to be regarded very seriously. No preaching today that does not address the fundamental human problem of universal sinfulness can be considered truly Christian preaching. Sadly, much preaching is still sub-Christian. Reinhold Niebuhr parodied some American preachers of his day for their vacuous sentimentality when they speak of 'a God without wrath who brought men without sin into a kingdom without judgement through the ministrations of a Christ without a cross'. The prayer of penitence begins the moment that the inner convicting voice says, 'You are the man; you are the woman.' We don't need one of those long checklists of possible sins that used to be popular sixty years ago in some Confirmation manuals to tell us what's wrong in our lives. It is likely that a conviction of moral failure will arise during prayer itself, but it might also come through our wandering thoughts. We should notice if there is a pattern in them, and consider whether these wandering thoughts lead back to a particular person or incident in our past. Is there any sin that we have not faced up to? We are brilliant at rationalising the down-side of our behaviour in situations that show us in a bad light, so we must try to be honest.

Often, the more relaxed we become in prayer the more likely we are to be conscious of unresolved sin. Quietly before God, we should allow the Holy Spirit to move into the subconscious areas of our minds so that he can identify and bring to the surface what we have been trying to hide for years. Although this can be a very disturbing experience, we should not shy away from it. I have been retired now for five years, and although it has brought new joys, one area of spiritual life has been discomforting. Being released from the attendant pressures and stresses of full-time ministry, I have found particular incidents and situations that I had practically forgotten now coming back into view. Many of these have been negative occasions when I have signally failed in a relationship, or have omitted to give the help that was needed at the time. Naturally, they have produced a strong sense of guilt and personal inadequacy. Having examined my previous life in this new light, I now realise how the failure and, yes, sin of the past has been excused, rationalised and even, on occasions, totally rejected. So I know, as well as anyone, how much I need to lay hold of the grace of our Lord Jesus Christ in his gifts of forgiveness and restoration.

There is every encouragement not to be afraid of this experience. When David heard that convicting word: 'You are the man', God was actually drawing close to him in mercy and grace. The Lord was speaking to him about his deepest problem because he wanted to solve it. He wanted David to see where the relationship had gone wrong so that it could be put right. We can be sure he wants to do the same for us. It's as though we go to a doctor who is also a close personal friend for an examination. He tells us that we have a major health problem, but if only we will trust him and allow him to treat us, we can be completely cured. We all need this treatment because, as the hymn writer reminds us, spiritual sickness is universal:

> And none, O Lord, have perfect rest;
> For none are wholly free from sin;
> And they who fain would serve thee best
> Are conscious most of wrong within.

Of all the books that I have ever read, I think the one that tried to take the problem and experience of sin most seriously was written in the 1930s. It was entitled, *For sinners only*. Possibly the anonymous author wanted his words to stand by themselves without being linked to any personal, identifiable situations. He argued that a small sense of sin means a small Christ. Sin, in fact, is a deadly force, for it 'Blinds, binds, multiplies, deadens and deafens us'. He defines sin as anything in my life which keeps me from God and from other people. He advocates examining our lives under the headings of the four absolutes which he defines as Honesty, Love, Purity and Unselfishness. 'Sin is a force,' he says, 'a mathematical force. It adds to a man's troubles, subtracts from his energies, multiplies his aches and pains, divides his mind, takes interest from his work, discounts his chances of success and squares his conscience'.

Penitence, then, finds a natural place in the prayer life of those who take sin seriously because they know God takes it seriously. The wrath of God is truly the reaction of holy love against sin. God is a holy God, but he cares so much for us. No one preached more profoundly about the love of God than William Temple. This is what he wrote about God's wrath:

> 'Terrible words! A sentimental and hedonistic generation tries to eliminate "wrath" from its conception of God. Of course, if "anger" and "wrath" are taken to mean the emotional reaction of an irritated self-concern, there is no such thing in God. But if God is holy love, and I am in any degree given to uncleanness or selfishness, then there is, in that degree, stark antagonism in God against me. And so long as I am disobedient the wrath of God continues.'

I think Reinhold Niebuhr would agree.

Let us suppose, then, that we have reached the point when we feel convicted of sin. This may have come about through the Holy Spirit working in our conscience, often through a word of Scripture, or by his speaking to us through another person. Or perhaps we have been brought up sharply as we've seen the consequences of our lamentable shortcomings. Someone has said, 'I never knew the meaning of selfishness until I saw tears in my mother's eyes.' The conviction may even have come through simply taking note of where our wandering thoughts and prayer time have led us. One way or another, light has penetrated some dark area of our lives, and we respond in repentance, which means that we turn back to God to receive his gift of forgiveness through Jesus Christ. We come back to God with the whole of our being, not just with our emotions but with our wills and

A **prayer** of cleansing

> Repentance is like the sea – a man can bathe in it at any hour.
> *Jewish saying*

minds also, recognising that the Holy Spirit is prompting us to take this step. We co-operate with what he initiates; it is God's work from beginning to end, all of his grace. This is brought home very powerfully in the Anglican *Book of Common Prayer*, in the pronouncement of the absolution at Morning and Evening Prayer with its plea to 'grant us true repentance and thy Holy Spirit'. This acknowledges that even our repentance is flawed and that we are totally dependent on God's grace from beginning to end to make it 'true repentance.' P. T. Forsythe saw this truth very clearly:

> 'It is, indeed, for Christ's sake that we are forgiven, but for the sake of a Christ who is the creator of our repentance and not only the proxy of our curse. And it is *to* our faith the grace is given, yet not *because* of our faith, which is no more perfect than our repentance. It is to nothing so poor as our faith that new life is given, but only to Christ on his cross and to us for his sake who is the creator and fashioner of both. Our justification rests on this atoning creative Christ alone.'

And although this act of repentance is normally for definite identifiable moments of moral and spiritual failure in our lives, it also needs to become a regular part of our prayer life. Dr Jim Packer writes:

> 'Repentance means turning from as much as you know of your sin to give as much as you know of yourself to as much as you know of your God, and as our knowledge grows at these three points so our practice of repentance has to be enlarged.'

All is of grace. God has provided the atoning sacrifice in Christ; so that as we repent 'the blood of Jesus his Son cleanses us from all sin' (1 John 1:7).

And so, in joyful recognition of the grace of God, we, in turn, want to show our gratitude by forgiving others. For as George Herbert has said, 'He who will not forgive another has broken the bridge over which he himself must pass.'

Finally, as you come to God in penitence and faith you may find it helpful to picture the scene in the upper room, just before the Last Supper. Jesus starts to wash the disciples' feet. Peter feels that this is totally inappropriate and is deeply embarrassed. But Jesus presses the issue: 'Unless I wash you, you have no share with me.' Suddenly, Peter sees his need. 'Lord, not my feet only but also my hands and my head' (John 13: 8, 9). In the same way, the Holy Spirit shows us our own need of total washing. We need washing of body, mind and spirit for our lives are flawed at every level. And our vision of Christ is that he can wash us spiritually in such a way that every part of life is cleansed. So we pray:

> Wash me, Lord –
> > I personally wish to receive this from you.
>
> Wash my feet, my heart, my head –
> > every part of me that is flawed.
>
> Wash me with water, blood, fire –
> > by your cleansing word
> > by your cleansing blood
> > by the fire of your cleansing Holy Spirit.

Chapter **eight**

Pleasure

At the heart of all prayer is a right relationship with God. It is a relationship which he has initiated and it is his idea from start to finish. It is all based on his grace. We can enjoy the privilege of prayer only because of this grace. We can begin to give prayer the priority that it should have in our lives only because God, in his grace, has given it priority in his relationship with us. All is of grace from start to finish. Our own prayer experience would be revolutionised if we could only begin each day with an overwhelming sense of God's grace.

The Westminster Confession states that 'the chief end of man is to glorify God and to enjoy him for ever'. This means that the whole of life is to revolve round God, and when every part of this relationship is right then we shall be able to enjoy him in the fulness of grace. The relationship begins here and now in time but extends into eternity. We can begin to enjoy our relationship with the holy, almighty God only when the first glimmerings of the meaning of grace dawn upon us.

How can an infinitely holy God own his sinful and antagonistic creation? Only because divine love, the quintessence of God's character, radiating out from Father, Son and Holy Spirit, longs for us to share in the perfect love relationship enjoyed in the blessed Trinity. There is nothing in rebellious creation that is innately loveable. And so grace is always surprising, always amazing, otherwise it would not be grace. Karl Barth has said, 'Only when grace is recognised to be incomprehensible is it grace.' God's grace is beyond definition because it is 'so amazing, so divine'. However, various writers have pointed towards the heart of the matter. W. H. Griffith Thomas, sometime principal of Wycliffe Hall, Oxford, wrote:

> 'Grace means more, far more than we can put into words, because it means nothing less than the infinite character of God himself. It includes mercy for the undeserving and unmerciful, help for the helpless and hopeless, redemption for the renegade and repulsive, love for the unloving and unlovely, kindness for the unkind and unthankful. And all this in full measure and overflowing abundance, because of nothing in the object and because of everything in the Giver, God himself.'

Human love – with the possible exception of parental love – flourishes when it is reciprocated and normally declines and dies when it is rejected. In his grace, God goes on loving despite being ignored, rejected or misunderstood. 'Grace is God's mysterious ongoing acceptance of me whatever my successes or failures', writes Charles Mahaney. And Philip Yancy puts it even more powerfully: 'Grace means that there is nothing we can do to make God love us more . . . . There is nothing we can do to make God love us less.'

Every morning we need to breathe in this atmosphere of grace so that our prayers are totally conditioned by the experience of

God's undeserved love. It has been said that 'all true religion starts with grace and ends with gratitude,' and that beautifully sums up the character of genuine prayer. When the whole of life starts with grace and ends with gratitude we are well on the way to enjoying God for ever. Because even more than words of asking, confessing and thanking, the most satisfying experience of prayer is the enjoyment of God's presence, now. This was surely at the heart of Jesus' prayer life. There was the daily prayer time when he would quietly leave the house and his sleeping disciples so that he could commune with his father in a field or on a hillside. Also, no doubt, each Sabbath was very meaningful for him, as Whittier suggests:

> O Sabbath rest by Galilee!
> O calm of hills above,
> Where Jesus knelt to share with thee
> The silence of eternity,
> Interpreted by love.

We can be sure Jesus was committing the tasks of each day and the activities of the week ahead to his Father, and in doing so was asking for guidance and strength. In faith, he was drawing on all the divine resources that he would need, as many sick and troubled people came to him for help and healing. But, supremely, he was just enjoying the presence of his Father; he was resting in his love and approval: 'You are my Son, the Beloved; with you I am well pleased' (Luke 3:22). In perfect unity and harmony between Father and Son, the relationship was complete.

We have seen how Jesus prayed for special help and guidance on important occasions, particularly at turning points of his ministry. The most notable example of this is when he prayed in the

Garden of Gethsemane with such agonised intensity that blood-flecked sweat ran down his face. And we have the actual record of how his petition changed from, in effect, 'Save me from this hour' to 'Father, your will be done'. But behind the actual words of petition or thanksgiving which Jesus used in his regular praying lay the daily enjoyment of his Father's presence. What an example for us in our daily prayer experience!

Straining after perfection will always produce stress and anxiety. Resting in Christ, abiding in him, allows the fruit of the Spirit to grow naturally at God's pace and in his way. Growth in holiness comes as we enjoy his grace and receive all things that come to us in life as his gift. 'Christ in you, the hope of glory' (Colossians 1:27) is Paul's summary of the mystery of divine life within us. We are to rest content, to dwell quietly in this glorious truth that God — Father, Son and Holy Spirit — lives within us. This means he is with us all the time and shares our life at every level: 'And remember, I am with you always, to the end of the age' (Matthew 28:20). The secret of the Christian life is having absolute confidence in Jesus' promise of his abiding presence.

This companionship, this simple friendship, as the Abbé de Tourville has said, should be accepted and trusted each day as God's gracious gift to us. Not examined so much as enjoyed. Examination simply means that we sense more and more how unworthy we are of it and this makes it more difficult to accept it as pure gift. 'Simply practise it; that is all.' All is of grace. Acts of external devotion have value; indeed, some people find them particularly helpful. But remember that they are 'only patterns, superimposed on this simple friendship'. The moment they get in the way of the spiritual relationship they should be revised or discontinued.

We are to speak to the Lord 'in the most homely words'. Of course, we all have different ways of expressing ourselves; so one of the great secrets of prayer is that we should talk with the Lord in the way that is entirely natural to us. He clearly does not

A **prayer** of fulfilment

> Bring us, O Lord God, at our last awakening
> into the house and gate of heaven,
> to enter that gate and dwell in that house
> where there shall be no darkness nor dazzling, but one equal light;
> no noise nor silence, but one equal music;
> no fears nor hopes, but one equal possession;
> no ends nor beginnings, but one equal eternity,
> in the habitations of thy majesty and thy glory for ever and ever. Amen.
> *JOHN DONNE (1571-1631)*

want us to put on a 'religious' act and use words that have no resonance in our daily lives. God is spirit and we must worship him in spirit and in truth, and that includes earthing our prayers in the truth and reality of our lives.

All is of grace. That is the final truth of our relationship to God to which prayer gives expression. Let Jesus' parable of the two sons have the last word as we allow the story to deepen our sense of God's grace.

For many people, prayer sounds a good idea when there is no immediate prospect of practising it. But the moment we become really serious and say, 'Now I will start,' all kinds of problems arise. The theory is great but the practice is difficult. We wonder if God will really be listening, let alone accepting and answering us. Suddenly, we don't feel in the mood; we may even feel that some or other problem disqualifies us from praying. Maybe we are all too conscious of some major moral blockage and fear that the Lord will turn his back on us. The younger son of Jesus' parable in Luke 15 had enormous problems about returning to his father, because he had left home under a cloud and then made such a mess of his life. He felt so guilty. Extreme circumstances made him decide to return, even though he could not conceive that his father would any longer accept him as his son. However, life in the bunkhouse with the farm workers would be infinitely preferable to eating pig-swill. No matter how great we perceive our difficulties in coming to God in prayer, we can gain reassurance from Jesus' illustration of our Father God's reaction in the parable of the prodigal son. Recognise and rejoice in the ten components of grace, both for him and for us:

First, day after day the father was looking far down the road to the distant horizon, watching eagerly for the first sign of his returning son. Perhaps each morning he climbed to the flat top of his farmhouse to gain the best vantage point to gaze through the heat-haze. Every morning he kept watch until one day he saw him, a long way off.

The second sign of grace was the father's individual, personal interest in the son who was special and who was coming home to him.

Thirdly, he had compassion on him. His father's heart of love overflowed in joy that his beloved son was coming back to him. All the weakness, failure and shame were as nothing compared with the overwhelming, infinite compassion of the father's love and acceptance of him.

And so, fourthly, he ran, ran to greet him while he was still a long way off. The returning son was still far distant and walking very slowly with blistered and bleeding feet, yet the elderly father ran all the way to welcome him.

When they met he embraced him. He put his arms round him. Nothing could have convinced the guilty son more fully of his acceptance by his father than this, the fifth sign of grace; and the sixth followed immediately as he kissed him. This was the kiss of love and of peace, the kiss of forgiveness. It was the sign that the relationship had been restored from the father's side, although, of course, it became a reality only when the young man took the decision to return home.

There then followed three further signs of grace which made the reconciliation and restoration absolute and complete. The father called for the robe that would cover the son's filthy condition. It was the father's gift (the apostle Paul will call it the robe of righteousness when he speaks of us in the prodigal son's place). He then placed a ring on his finger, symbolising the renewal of the family covenant. The young man might not have felt like a son; everything about his recent life denied it, but the ring proved that the relationship had been re-established. He had only to look at it, to finger it, and all his misgivings vanished. The ring was fact; he was forgiven. And then again, the father called for shoes for his feet, because a son must not go barefoot. Shoes meant that he could begin to walk around his home and enjoy his new life.

Finally, there was the tenth sign of grace as the father could hardly contain his joy. It was so complete and overflowing that he wanted to share it with everyone. And so friends, neighbours and servants were all invited to celebrate with him. The party began so joyfully and was clouded only by the arrival of the older brother. Having worked dutifully, responsibly and painstakingly from dawn till dusk, he was infuriated by all that was taking place in the house. All that extravagant, emotional fuss over his disgraceful, family-shaming brother! What was his father thinking of to go over the top in such a sickening way?

And so the last, sad, inconclusive conversation takes place outside the house, in the farmyard. The older boy's bitterness and jealousy erupt as he reveals that he has no concept of grace whatsoever.

> 'Listen! For all these years I have been working like a slave for you, and I have never disobeyed your command; yet you have never given me even a young goat so that I might celebrate with my friends. But when this son of yours came back, who has devoured your property with prostitutes, you killed the fatted calf for him!' (Luke 15:29, 30).

In reply, his father assures him that he has loved him just as much all these years and freely shared everything with him, 'Son, you are always with me, and all that is mine is yours' (Luke l5:31). Tragically, his son has never recognised this and so never enjoyed it. Poor man! His life is totally bound up with his heavy, plodding work routine, day in and day out, toiling away on the family farm. His whole existence is confined within his introverted sense of a daily grind — no joy, no grace, no experience of the wonderful gift he is inheriting as the son of such a caring and generous father. He is constantly thinking about earning his father's favour and just cannot see that everything around him can be enjoyed as a gift.

We ourselves can look inward and downward, seeing only

what life owes us because of what we reckon we deserve. Or we can choose to look around us and upwards, catching a vision of God's grace: 'All that is mine is yours'.

Grace is the conditioning atmosphere; indeed, it is the very oxygen of prayer. And so our actual practice of prayer helps us to appreciate our wonderful riches in Christ Jesus here and now, and points us forward into the limitless future as we enjoy him for ever.

> 'Jesus, priceless treasure,
> Source of purest pleasure,
> Truest friend to me;
> Long my heart hath panted,
> Till it well-nigh fainted,
> Thirsting, Lord, for thee.
> I will suffer nought to hide thee,
> Ask for nought beside thee.
> Hence, all thoughts of sadness!
> For the Lord of gladness,
> Jesus, enters in:
> Those who love the Father,
> Though the storms may gather,
> Still have peace within;
> Yea, whate'er we here must bear,
> Still in thee lies purest pleasure,
> Jesus, priceless treasure.'
>
> (from *Jesus, priceless treasure* by J. Franck)

Chapter **nine**

Presence

The end of the twentieth century saw many churches experiencing spiritual renewal. Worship became more vibrant and enthusiastic and, to some observers, rather noisy. At the same time, the Spirit was moving other Christians to find a new quietness in their inner lives and a desire to discover more of the secrets of meditative prayer. Surely this experience of quiet, reflective prayer is as much the work of the Holy Spirit as the more extrovert and exuberant expressions of praise.

Although I have been interested in practising the presence of God since my theological training in the 1950s I have used it consistently only since the late eighties. At that time I felt the need to make space each day for a period of meditative prayer.

At the heart of this spiritual exercise is an emphasis on the need for stillness of body and mind. This may sound simple enough, but many of us in practice find it quite difficult; for even when the body is still, our thoughts are more than capable of wandering off in different directions. This is because, even when the conscious mind seeks quietness and stillness, the subconscious mind is often restless. Of all forms of prayer this is the one that can supremely affect both mental levels. The human mind is rather like an iceberg, in that the conscious part is one seventh above the surface while the subconscious mind is the six sevenths below. As meditative prayer can penetrate both levels of the mind, we can understand how this form of prayer can influence us deeply.

A **prayer** for Christ's presence

> May the strength of God pilot us.
> May the power of God preserve us.
> May the wisdom of God insruct us.
> May the hand of God direct us.
> May the shield of God defend us.
> May the host of God guard us
> against the snares of evil
> and the temptations of the world.
> May Christ be with us, Christ before us,
> Christ in us, Christ over us.
> May thy salvation, O Lord,
> be always ours this day and for evermore.
> ST PATRICK *(389-c. 461)*

If stillness is of such importance, how can we experience it when our lives are in any way stressed or discordant? First, we need to sit quietly by ourselves in reasonable comfort. If we are conscious of tension in arms, legs, neck or head, it can be helpful to flex the muscles in those areas and then to release them.

But, of course, the mind and spirit need to be quietened even more than the body. We need to use phrases or short sentences which enable us to relax in the presence of God and to enjoy the reality of his love. Personally, I believe that these 'prayer phrases' *should be based on Scripture.* This will safeguard against feeding our minds with ideas other than truths of divine revelation. This is particularly important when we recall that we are feeding not only our conscious minds but the deeper area of our subconscious as well. We hear today of the dangers of subliminal advertising through which we can be unconsciously subjected to manipulation. To ensure that God's truth is the source of every influence, I use only Bible passages in meditation. However, it is important to use them in a form that easily

A **prayer** for true silence

Love silence, even in the mind;
for thoughts are to that as words to the body, troublesome:
much speaking as much thinking, spends.
True silence is the rest of the mind;
and is to the spirit what sleep is the the body,
nourishment and refreshment.
WILLIAM PENN (1644-1718)

resonates in the mind so that they can be silently repeated without tension for a period of time. Today, with many Bible translations to choose from, I tend to use one in which the words have a flowing rhythm. Frequently I find myself returning to the Authorised Version, or a modern translation that is based on it.

Stillness leads to a realisation of the presence of God: at its essence this is the 'I : Thou' relationship which was described in Chapter 3. We rest in Christ, dwell in him and he in us. In so doing we allow God to release within us spiritual powers which promote peace, wholeness and spiritual growth. But our primary objective is simply to be in the presence of God. Once we have begun to centre down we can use some specific Bible verses to help us become more aware of that divine presence.

We have already mentioned that, inevitably, our minds will wander whatever form of prayer we're using, and this problem will certainly arise in meditative prayer. We should not be discouraged, but as soon as we realise that we have lost our theme we should simply cut off the digression and pull back to the original Bible verses.

One short chapter cannot possibly do justice to this deeply satisfying form of prayer which certainly helps many people. I have given a fuller treatment of the subject in my *Spirit Borne* – an introduction to biblical meditation (published by The Bible Reading Fellowship 1996) and here I quote a paragraph from it:

> 'It is important to set out the truly objective facts about meditation as many people have the idea that it's a pious, subjective exercise that inadequate people undertake as an escape from reality. It is quite the reverse. It brings the glorious transcendent reality of God into our experience in a remarkable way. It is a spiritual exercise that can benefit all Christians and it may well be especially powerful for the many people today who are subject to stress. It also helps us to overcome the perennial problem of translating head knowledge into heart knowledge, of transforming the purely cerebral into the warmth of

personal experience. As the classic devotional writers tell us, it enables us to possess our possessions in Christ and to become what we already truly are in him' (page 11).

If, then, you were to put the direct question to me: 'What is the point of meditative prayer?' I would answer with three reasons. First, it deepens our experience of the presence of God. Secondly, it releases divine power within us through the Holy Spirit. Thirdly, it enables us to experience some of the greatest truths of the Bible at a deeper and more personal level. Simply by holding some great scriptural promise or truth in our minds over a period of time, we enhance our appreciation of it. Of course, it's important to start with an understanding of the Scripture, and so we need to look at the biblical context. At this preliminary stage we are using our conscious minds analytically. As we grasp the meaning of the text we are using, we first approve it and then trust it. In so doing we move from the intellectual to the spiritual and devotional. As we accept these truths by faith, we trust and rejoice in them. Through the repetition of chosen verses in the conscious mind, we are beginning to engage the subconscious mind also. It is at this point that the real benefits of meditative prayer begin to impinge upon us because the Holy Spirit is working within us at this deeper, hidden, level.

So now let us put this into practice. Begin to centre down and become still in God's presence. Listen to divine commands:

Be still in my presence

Be still and know that I am God (Psalm 46:10)

But be conscious also of Christ's promise:

Be sure I am with you always (Matthew 28:20)

God speaks to us but we also speak back to him. So we can now make our response:

For you alone my soul in silence waits (Psalm 62:1)

As we wait on God, in quiet trust, we begin to move towards the focal point where we rest in Christ according to his invitation in John 15:4 and 5:

Rest in Christ

Dwell in him,

he in us

or, if we wish to make the experience more personal, say:

Dwell in you – you in me

We can now move into using the Bible verses or prayer phrase which we find is appropriate to our particular need. I am aware that some suggest that we use one and the same scriptural verses each day. My own preference is to use a variety of phrases in order that different personal needs can be addressed.

So let's get started. Read through the first six verses of chapter two in Paul's letter to the Ephesians and see how he speaks of Christ's identification with us in his death, resurrection and ascension. Because we are incorporated into Christ himself by his plan of grace we can say:

Dead, raised, reign with Christ.

Now turn to the book of Isaiah and one of the great promises which speak of God's saving and strengthening power:

'For thus says the Lord God, the Holy One of Israel; In returning and rest shall ye be saved; in quietness and in confidence shall be your strength: and ye would not' (Isaiah 30:15, KJV).

We must note that this promise is conditional on our turning back to God. Of course, in one sense, every time we start to meditate we are meeting that condition and so the promise is for us.

Another passage can be used at those times when we feel

overwhelmed by our sense of powerlessness in the face of our circumstances. We feel we cannot cope; we cannot see a way out of the difficulty; it is all too much! But then we remember that God has promised strength for whatever he allows in our lives. Paul gives us this truth in Philippians 4:13 which suggests this meditation:

I can do all things – through Christ –

who strengthens – me

This prayer phrase can be extended as we recall that the people of Jesus' day said that he did all things well (Mark 7:37) and that he has promised to make all things new (Revelation 21:5).

I can't –

but God can –

Let go –

let God –

he – does – all – things – well

he – makes – all – things – new

Paul further emphasises this truth in one of God's greatest promises. You will find it in 2 Corinthians 12:9:

My grace – is all – you need –

My power – perfected – in weakness

The spiritual resources that we find in Christ are a constant source of inspiration. When we consider all that God has done for us in Christ, as expressed in Paul's words in Romans 8:32, we shall find the answer to the question he is posing liberating. The full verse reads:

'He that spared not his own Son, but delivered him up for us all, how shall he not with him also freely give us all things?' (KJV.)

And the prayer phrase for our meditation becomes:

How shall – he not – with him – also –

freely – give us – all things

This is exactly what the father said to the older brother in Jesus' story of the prodigal son (Luke 15:31) and which can be turned into the prayer phrase:

All that – I have – is yours

Paul has this truth in mind when he sums up his second great prayer in the letter to the Ephesians (3:19) as he desires that we should be

filled – with all – the fullness – of God

At the centre of the prayer – that we should all be filled with all the fulness of God – is divine love, and it helps here to have a hymnbook at hand to reinforce the power of the prayer phrase. I have mine open now at a hymn which John Wesley translated from the German of Paul Gerhardt:

> Jesus, thy boundless love to me
> No thought can reach, no tongue declare;
> O knit my thankful heart to thee,
> And reign without a rival there:
> Thine wholly, thine alone, I am;
> Be thou alone my constant flame.
>
> O grant that nothing in my soul
> May dwell, but thy pure love alone;
> O may thy love possess me whole,
> My joy, my treasure, and my crown:
> Strange flames far from my heart remove;
> My every act, word, thought, be love.

> O Love, how cheering is thy ray!
> All pain before thy presence flies,
> Care, anguish, sorrow, melt away,
> Wher'er thy healing beams arise:
> O Jesus, nothing may I see,
> Nothing desire, or seek, but thee.

Finally, for any who lack assurance of faith, here is a prayer phrase in which we need to hear the Lord himself speaking directly to us, Jesus addressing us personally. It comes from John's gospel, 6:37, where Jesus promises:

He (she) – who comes – to me –

I never – cast out

Whenever a text particularly speaks to you, write it down, play with the words or look them up in various translations until you get them into a form which is easily memorised. Be careful not to change the meaning in any way. As you revolve them around your mind, allow them to speak to you as you relax in the presence of God and trust the truth that they contain.

Finish by radiating that truth into the lives of others around you.

Chapter **ten**

Pattern

Jesus was praying in a certain place; and after he had finished, one of his disciples said to him, ' "Lord, teach us to pray, as John taught his disciples." He said to them, "When you pray, say: Father, hallowed be your name . . ." ' (Luke 11:1, 2).

It would be fascinating to learn what John the Baptist taught his disciples about the art of prayer. Many of Jesus' own followers had originally been with John and had absorbed his teaching on prayer. But it seems that it was Jesus' own example which prompted the request here. It sounds as though the disciples were not so much praying with Jesus as actually observing him at prayer, and what they saw clearly impressed them.

It has been suggested that the prayer Jesus gave to his disciples was one that developed out of his own experience. While 'forgive us our trespasses' clearly cannot apply to the sinless One, it is not impossible that some elements of the prayer arose out of Jesus' own experiences. Perhaps he reduced the words to a simple formula which could be easily memorised, but the profundity of the subject matter goes to the heart of his own ministry and the personal relationship with his Father. Anyone who has tried praying this prayer of Jesus' over an extended period of time – say, half an hour – will know that these simple sentences have unlimited spiritual possibilities.

Each sentence of the prayer reveals how Jesus' mind was working as his ministry developed, and illustrates how his followers can continue to pray until the end of time.

In the gospels, the Lord's Prayer is recorded twice, Matthew's version in the Sermon on the Mount being the longer of the two (Matthew 6:9-13). The form I give here is the one which I use when trying to pray this 'pattern' prayer in an unhurried manner.

Abba Father

What a privilege to be able to address our heavenly Father in this way. We have already seen that Paul gives us the encouragement to do just this when he writes, 'Because you are children, God has sent the Spirit of his Son into our hearts, crying, "Abba! Father!" ' (Galatians 4:6).

Since we have the assurance of his fatherly concern and understanding, we trust that we can 'cast all our anxieties on him, because he cares for us' (see 1 Peter 5:7). Alongside all the warmth and love of our caring Abba Father we must also recognise that he is God-almighty, the holy One, all powerful, all wise, all knowing, and so it is fitting that we should immediately be seriously concerned for the honour of his name.

Your name hallowed

We acknowledge that absolute holiness belongs to our Father God. Our prayer is centred on him: he is the great Creator and we are his creatures. Yes, through Jesus Christ we have become adopted sons and daughters of God, but we must never forget where we have come from, for this emphasises our present standing and privileges all the more.

In the Old Testament, holiness was revealed to his people supremely through Moses. That the Lord demanded the moral holiness enshrined in the Ten Commandments was a revolutionary concept when compared with the moral standards of all other religions of the Near East at that time. And the holiness of God was doubly reinforced by the sacrificial system that Moses introduced to the people. All the personal sin and guilt offerings were summed up each year on the great Day of Atonement, when the High Priest would enter the Holy of Holies at the heart of the Tabernacle to offer sacrificial blood for the whole nation. This blood was sprinkled on the holy Ark of the Covenant in the presence of God. The High Priest had bells sewn on his vestments so that by their tinkling the people would know that he had not died as he was carrying out his awesome ceremonial duties, hidden from them behind the heavy curtain – the 'veil of the temple'.

Our first and most important petition is that God's holy name should be honoured and reverenced. But as we can come to God the Father only through our Lord Jesus Christ in the Holy Spirit, we now use the name of God in trinity. And because Jesus Christ uncovers the nature of God to us and then gives us access to the Father, we naturally want Jesus' name to be honoured, revered and adored. I wonder how much it really hurts us when his name is defiled through ridicule or blasphemy.

Your Kingdom come

Jesus came to inaugurate the kingdom of God. And since his ascension, we recognise him as King. God's reign comes when

Jesus is recognised as Saviour and Lord and we welcome him by faith. So here our prayer is that Jesus may be accepted, trusted and followed as Saviour and Lord by all people. Put in practical terms, our prayer needs to move out in concentric circles.

Start with your own family and close friends, then radiate out to your neighbours and the people you work with. Then embrace a much wider circle of people in community and national life, moving, finally, out into the world. No doubt you are beginning to feel overwhelmed by the scale of this intercession, so try to pray realistically, within your faith. Don't lose the sense of prayer as a privilege, and remember that it always releases divine power. Try to discover by experiment where you should place the prime emphasis as you pray for the coming of God's reign. Be guided by the Holy Spirit who will bring people and situations into your mind; focus particularly on these.

Your will be done

Here we pray that all who honour Christ Jesus as Lord will, in all practical ways, know and follow his will. God has a plan for our lives and it is vitally important that we follow it, not only in the big things, but in the smaller details of each day as well. We want him to have the casting vote in every decision we have to make and so, naturally, this needs to be a daily prayer. We are praying that the 'still, small voice' of the Holy Spirit will be picked up in every situation: 'And when you turn to the right or when you turn to the left, your ears shall hear a word behind you, saying, "This is the way; walk in it" ' (Isaiah 30:21).

At the heart of all guidance God's will is working in our wills. The will is at the centre of human life, even beyond the working of the intellect or emotions. When we align our wills with his will, then the outworking of his plan for our lives brings peace. 'Your will is my peace' is a good sentence to recall at the beginning of each day.

The Christian marriage service illustrates this truth forcibly. In this the bride and groom do not publicly state that they think their marriage is a brilliant idea, or that they feel emotionally good about it. Rather, they affirm to each other, 'I will', for the will is the final controlling factor in life. The willing brings the commitment.

What we pray for ourselves we also ask for the whole Church – that God's will be done in every way, in all situations: the people of God neither rushing ahead nor lagging behind his will. We should want what God wants rather than putting our own wishes at the top of the agenda. Wouldn't it make a difference to church meetings if the chairperson started with the question, 'What does God most want us to be or do today?' and then called for five minutes' silent reflection?

> Breathe on me, breath of God
> Until my heart is pure
> Until with Thee I will one will
> To do and to endure
>
> EDWIN HATCH

Give daily bread

Here we pray that God will provide the real necessities for daily life: food, shelter, clothing, work, and so on. In fact, everything that makes ordinary everyday life possible and satisfying. 'Daily bread' suggests the basic minimum requirement for our existence, so it would seem that Jesus intends us to make this a daily prayer. No doubt this part of the Lord's Prayer reflects the hardships of life in his own time. I wonder if those of us who live under very different conditions turn this petition into thanksgiving, as we recognise that we have sufficient (even abundance) not only for each day but probably for weeks ahead. In being thankful, we are acknowledging that everything we are, or possess, comes from God's grace. In his divine providence he has ordained that we should be born at a time and under circumstances that have brought untold blessings to us. Through the educational opportunities available in our day, we have the possibility of realising our full potential. He has ordered the events of our lives so that we can benefit from the gifts that others bestow upon us — privileges which come through our upbring-

A **prayer** for a vision

> O God, our Judge and Saviour,
> set before us the vision of thy holiness,
> pierce our self-contentment with the shafts of thy burning love,
> and let that love consume in us
> all that hinders us from perfect service to thy cause;
> for as thy holiness is our judgement,
> so are thy wounds our salvation.
> WILLIAM TEMPLE (1881-1944)

ing, marriage or friendships. And so the phrase 'daily bread' has vast significance, whether we use it in petition or thanksgiving.

Simply at the physical level there is still so much more to it because we are praying in the plural and we recognise that although we have been greatly blessed many others have not. And so this prayer reaches out to all who struggle for survival, the many in our world for whom daily bread, literally, would be a luxury. And in our thoughts we link all those who are engaged in trying to alleviate need by any means, be they individuals, aid agencies or governments.

Jesus reminds us that Scripture tells us that we should not live by bread alone but by every word which proceeds from the mouth of God (Matthew 4:4). So we recognise in this petition that we need spiritual food each day every bit as much as we need bodily nourishment. We've no doubt been horrified to see television pictures showing conditions in countries experiencing famine. My local church has a particular link with the Sudan, and it is harrowing to see the famines that regularly ravage that land. Yet how many in our own country are trying to exist spiritually on starvation rations? Just as the human body needs between 2,000-2,500 calories a day in order to function properly, so the spirit needs to be nourished with spiritual food. Now for most of us, those 'spiritual calories' are freely available and can be assimilated as we worship with other Christians, in word and sacrament, in Christian fellowship, and in regular prayer and study of the Bible. If, however, we deliberately choose to deprive ourselves of the spiritual calories needed to keep our inner lives healthy, we are inviting trouble in the same way as when we neglect to nourish our physical bodies. Just as we are prone to disease and depression through poor diet, so we can become spiritually weak and lethargic, shaky in our faith and unsure of daily guidance, if we neglect to feed on God, and this can lead to our losing the sense of his presence in our lives. We need, therefore, both physical and spiritual provision every day.

Forgive our sins – as we forgive

I have dealt with this part of the Lord's prayer in the chapter on penitence; and so do not propose to say anything further now, except to add this thought. Jesus included these two petitions in his prayer, although he himself did not have any personal sin to confess. And at his baptism he voluntarily accepted a rite which signified repentance for sin. In this he was identifying with fallen humanity, and it was a vicarious act that found its climax when he hung on the cross at Calvary. So it is in this sense that Jesus could pray, 'forgive our sins' each day. And in his fully human nature he would have had good reason to pray, 'as we forgive'. After all, his many enemies were constantly questioning his authority, seeking to undermine his ministry, blackening his character and plotting to destroy him. Surely, it was because Jesus was always ready to forgive his enemies that he was able to speak so directly and trenchantly to them.

Lead us Lord; we trust you

For many of us this petition is the most difficult part of the Lord's Prayer. 'Lead us not into temptation' is the older version, whereas scholars tell us that the translation 'do not bring us to the time of trial' better expresses the original meaning. I think the key scripture on this subject is from James 1:12-16:

> 'Blessed is anyone who endures temptation. Such a one has stood the test and will receive the crown of life that the Lord has promised to those who love him. No one, when tempted, should say, 'I am being tempted by God'; for God cannot be tempted by evil and he himself tempts no one. But one is tempted by one's own desire, being lured and enticed by it; then, when that desire has

conceived, it gives birth to sin, and that sin, when it is fully grown, gives birth to death. Do not be deceived, my beloved.'

This passage makes it quite clear that temptation is not sin. It is a spiritual attack on us, but it is only when the lust at the heart of temptation has been conceived that we actually commit the sin. The essence of temptation is the desire to have our own way and not God's. It is to place ourselves at the centre of our world instead of him. It is simply our failure to put our trust in him. We decide to walk by sight and not by faith.

A good illustration of the way in which human nature can give way to temptation is seen in what happened to the Israelites when they had escaped from Egypt under Moses. Roughly a year after crossing the Red Sea they were poised to enter the promised land. Before pushing forward, Moses, like any sensible leader, decided to send in a reconnaissance party. He detailed twelve men, highly responsible and leaders of tribes, and told them to enter Canaan secretly and spy out the land. After several weeks this party returned and gave their report. They agreed unanimously that it was a beautiful and fertile country. They also reported that the cities were strongly defended and in some parts they had seen men of huge stature. When it came to the final verdict, their unanimity collapsed: ten out of the twelve reasoned that the country was too strongly defended for an attack to be attempted and it was, therefore, out of the question to move forward. But the other two spies disagreed strongly. Joshua and Caleb had seen all that the others had, but had reached a very different conclusion. God had commanded them to enter the land and he had promised to be with them, and so:

'Caleb quieted the people before Moses, and said, "Let

us go up at once and occupy it, for we are well able to overcome it" ' (Numbers 13:30).

Sadly, however, the majority verdict threw the Israelites into a panic. Moses and Aaron were no longer able to control them and there was even a hysterical suggestion that it would be better to go back to Egypt. In such a situation of confusion, turmoil and fear it must have required great courage and faith to see the true problem:

'And Joshua son of Nun and Caleb son of Jephunneh, who were among those who had spied out the land, tore their clothes and said to all the congregation of the Israelites, "The land that we went through as spies is an exceedingly good land. If the Lord is pleased with us, he will bring us into this land and give it to us, a land that flows with milk and honey. Only, do not rebel against the Lord; and do not fear the people of the land, for they are no more than bread for us; their protection is removed from them, and the Lord is with us; do not fear them" ' (Numbers 14:6-10).

At the heart of all temptation there is the insidious inner voice whispering that God is not to be trusted, that his promises are not true and that his way is too difficult. It is a direct attack on our faith and a challenge to face up to where our real loyalty lies. When we have honestly done that, then we can pray, 'Lead us, Lord; we trust you'.

Deliver me from evil

We pray to be delivered from all evil and to be delivered from the evil one; and we can do this with confidence because Jesus has won the victory. Whatever negative, antagonistic, hostile forces are arrayed against us, Jesus Christ is stronger. This prayer phrase is both a petition and an affirmation. The ultimate power is in the name of Jesus. Peter's preaching in the early chapters of the Acts of the Apostles specifically asserts that Jesus' name has final authority for healing (Acts 3:6) and for salvation (Acts 4:12). And it is in the name of Jesus, the ascended Saviour, Redeemer and royal High Priest, that we pray to be delivered from all evil and from the malign spiritual power who manipulates every evil force in our world. Jesus is the 'stronger man' who can defend his own against all comers.

As followers of Jesus, we are not taken out of the world; the battle will continue until the Lord returns, but we have to learn to live in Jesus Christ's victory. That victory was won through the offering of his perfect, sinless life on Calvary's cross, and then gloriously affirmed by his resurrection and triumphant return to heaven.

In the first eight chapters of his letter to the Romans, Paul shows how Jesus' victory can be transposed into our own lives. It is Jesus Christ himself who makes it all possible. In Romans 8 we learn that it is the Holy Spirit who makes the victory actual and experiential. Paul tries to visualise every conceivable adversity that could overpower and throw us down in defeat:

> 'Who will separate us from the love of Christ? Will hardship, or distress, or persecution, or famine, or nakedness, or peril, or sword?' (Romans 8:35).

And we can picture what Paul had in mind, as we know from our church history something of the suffering endured by God's people down through the ages. But perhaps not everyone is aware that there have been as many martyrs for Christ's cause in the twentieth century as suffered death in the worst persecutions in the Roman Empire of Diocletian or Decius. Were these heroes of faith defeated by an enemy too strong to withstand? Absolutely not, according to Paul, who goes on to answer his own question with the ringing affirmation:

> 'No, in all things we are more than conquerors through him who loved us' (Romans 8:37).

And so we are able, with Paul, to move to the glorious conclusion of this victory:

> 'For I am convinced that neither death, nor life, nor angels, nor rulers, nor things present, nor things to come, nor powers, nor height, nor depth, nor anything else in all creation, will be able to separate us from the love of God in Christ Jesus our Lord'
> (Romans 8:38, 39).

Kingdom – Power – Glory

The final ascription in the pattern prayer is a pure act of adoration and praise. It follows inevitably from the truth of the victory of Jesus over all evil power. Just as the prayer began with adoration, 'Your name be hallowed', so it ends on exactly the same note: 'For yours is the kingdom, the power and the glory'. We have come to the Father, through the Son, in the Spirit, and recalled how the pattern prayer was first regularly prayed on earth by the Son, to the Father, in the Spirit. Whatever else it may mean, when we pray the Lord's Prayer as Jesus did, then we must surely be praying supremely in the Spirit. This is the most powerful prayer that can ever be used. Don't spoil it by praying it too quickly. And finally, let everything be gathered up in wonder, love and praise.

Chapter **eleven**

Psalms

While all psalms are examples of Hebrew poetry, not all of them are prayers. And even the ones which clearly address God in an attitude of prayer are not all suitable for personal devotional use. The examples we shall be looking at have been selected in the hope that they will encourage and enrich our own prayers. In the Old Testament, all of these are attributed to King David. However, as the title was not part of the original psalm, we cannot be sure of Davidic authorship. We should keep in mind the oral tradition of that period through which knowledge was largely received; stories, poetry and songs would have been learned by heart and handed down from one generation to the next, with the inevitability of some variation from the original work. Also, we need to remember that most psalms had probably passed through a number of editorial stages before being finally honed for use in temple worship.

The doubt about authorship, or the evidence for later amendment, is most clear when there is a mention of the Temple at Jerusalem which is known to have been built by Solomon many years after David's death (see for example, Psalm 79).

There is a devotional purpose, however, in choosing psalms that are attributed to David. Many of them probably do go back to him in their original form. This means that there is the likelihood that they were based on his own personal experience. Perhaps it helps if we first picture David as a teenage shepherd out on the hills with his sheep, beginning to compose his early lyrics over the campfire. After all, many of us have had a go at poetic scribbling in our formative years. Following his victory over Goliath, David became a popular army commander in the service of King Saul, and we know that he used his musical gift to calm Saul's paranoid depressions, accompanying his songs on the harp. No doubt he slipped in some of his own compositions among the traditional Hebrew folk songs and spirituals.

A little later, during the years in the Judean wilderness when David was hunted as a fugitive, he would have had time on his hands to indulge his poetic gift. I sense that many psalms that speak of his enemies and their malicious lies had their origin in this period. Possibly, when he was King he worked the poems over again, being by then even more sensitive to the subtle attacks of his many enemies.

Inevitably, a few of the psalms are directly related to one or other of those two personal disasters in David's life, the Bathsheba incident and the rebellion of Absalom.

Because of their devotional nature we can make use of these psalms in our own prayers. We shall see how they address God and reveal the true feelings of the psalmist at the time. We will also look to see which are the words used in adoration, confession, thanksgiving or intercession. Above all, we need to sense that here is a man in deadly earnest about his faith. David knows himself to be in the presence of God; and because of his trustful relationship with his Lord he is able to speak as he really feels. He can pour out his innermost emotions, confident that God will interpret them correctly. And let's be quite honest: there are times when the psalmists complain bitterly to God about his apparent indifference to their predicament:

'O God, do not keep silence; do not hold your peace or be still, O God!' (Psalm 83:1).

'I am weary with my crying; my throat is parched. My eyes grow dim with waiting for my God' (Psalm 69:3).

'Rouse yourself! Why do you sleep, O Lord? Awake, do not cast us off forever!' (Psalm 44:23).

'Rise up, O Lord, in your anger; lift yourself up against the fury of my enemies: awake, O my God; you have appointed a judgment' (Psalm 7:6).

Lord Coggan, former Archbishop of Canterbury, in his recent exposition of the Psalms (*The People's Bible Commentary*,

A **prayer** of worship

O God, You have bidden us worship you
with the sound of the trumpet, with psaltery and harp,
with stringed instruments and organs,
and also to be glad in you and to shout for joy:
Help us to contrive by all means to set forth
your most worthy praise,
that our art may be tuned to the glory of God;
for the sake of him whose voice is as the sound of many waters,
Jesus Christ, our Lord.

JOHN R. W. STOTT (1921–)

published by The Bible Reading Fellowship), helps us to appreciate the intensity of the psalmists' feelings:

> 'God is spirit (John 4:24). But we have bodies, and if we are to speak with any reality about God we can only do so if we use physical terms. Thus we speak of God's eyes being open (Psalm11:4), his arms outstretched (Psalm 44:3), his nostrils emitting smoke (Psalm 18:8), and so on. Perhaps one of the most daring uses of such language is to speak of God as asleep. Sleep implies inactivity and inability to act. Sometimes, with great boldness and in extreme suffering, the psalmists charge God with being asleep – this would be blasphemous if it were not said by people in agony!' (Commentary on Psalm 7.)

The amazing thing is that these words are contained in Holy Scripture and they show that if the relationship is right then we are permitted to say them. Once again, we are back to the principle of practising the presence of God. When that is a reality, then everything else that follows is permissible.

So now let us examine a few of David's psalms to see how we may be encouraged in our own prayer life.

Psalm 5

This psalm is probably one of David's morning prayers – see verse 3. his approach to God is first stated negatively (verses 4-6), because he knows that God will not hear him if he deliberately harbours sin in his life. But then the positive is affirmed as he basks in the Lord's faithful love:

> 'But I, through the abundance of your steadfast love,
> will enter your house' (verse 7).

David addresses God in various ways: in verse 2 as 'my King

and my God'; in verse 10, as 'O God'. He bows in awe before the living God in an attitude of reverence balanced by confidence. He is praying with some emotion because he speaks of 'sighing' in verse 1 and he 'cries' to God in verse 2. The problems he faces seem to be the plots of his enemies who are spreading malicious lies about him. Words that distort the truth were as damaging and hurtful then as they can be today! David reacts robustly, believing that he is truly seeking to implement God's righteous will in his kingdom. He is in no doubt that the enemies who rebel against him are now also rebelling against God (verse 10).

What, then, does David actually ask of God in this early morning prayer? His request is for guidance to steer him through a day which he fully expects to be beset by difficulties:

> 'Lead me, O Lord, in your righteousness because of my enemies; make your way straight before me' (verse 8).

And he continues in prayer that his actions and motives may be vindicated against the distortions of his enemies. Throughout this prayer, David is trusting in God's righteousness and mercy so that evil attacks on him and on God's purposes may be exposed and then collapse.

In the last two verses, David widens his prayer into an embracing, corporate blessing upon all in his kingdom who truly follow the Lord:

> 'Let all who take refuge in you rejoice; let them ever sing for joy. Spread your protection over them, so that those who love your name may exult in you. For you bless the righteous, O Lord; you cover them with favour as with a shield' (verses 11, 12).

What a wonderful prayer to take with us into the life of each day!

Psalm 13

Dr Graham Scroggie gives this psalm the succinct subtitle, 'From sighing to singing', and this well describes its change of mood. Like a number of psalms, it starts in the depths and ends in the heights. Although, it must be admitted, a few show the reverse process. This suggests that we must be alert to the changes of emotion that mark our own prayer experience and recognise them as significant. Here, David is in despair and four times calls out to God, 'How long, O Lord?' But even in the depths of misery, he is still conscious of the Lord, 'my God' (verse 3). There is deep feeling here; possibly David is seriously ill – certainly he is depressed:

> 'How long must I bear pain in my soul, and have sorrow in my heart all day long?' (verse 2a).

And, perhaps worst of all, God seems distant and silent:

> 'How long will you hide your face from me?'
> (verse 1b).

David is so sick and depressed that he wonders if he will die (verse 3b). And he knows full well that his death would give his enemies the greatest satisfaction. His removal from the scene would be just what they wanted (verse 4).

His petition, then, seems to be a reflection on how long he must go on suffering while God remains silent. He longs to have an answer that will reassure him of God's approval and restore to him the sense of his presence.

Possibly, the last two verses were added later when his situation had changed. his faltering faith – barely kept alive during the dark days – is vindicated. The sense of God's constant, steadfast love has come flooding back to him and his heart sings in praise of the Lord's saving power.

Donald Coggan traces the movement of this psalm:
> 'Psalm 13 begins with protest (verses 1 and 2), "How long, Lord?" goes on to prayer (verses 3 and 4), "Look now, Lord my God, and answer me;" ends with praise (verses 5 and 6), "I shall sing to the Lord, for he has granted all my desire." It is a good progression. Possibly a pattern for our prayer life?' (Commentary on Psalm 13).

Psalm 25

In this psalm David prays with wholehearted trust in God's faithfulness. That beautiful phrase, 'your steadfast love', comes up again and again. It means that God will never go back on his love for his people or break his covenant promises. He is utterly dependable and he does not 'blow hot and cold'. Since he is so faithful, the nation, for its part, must trust him fully.

David is in serious trouble. He has deep spiritual problems within, and at the same time has to contend with the physical enemies who are seeking to discredit him by false accusation. He relies on God's covenant grace to bring answers to his problems:
> 'To you, O Lord, I lift up my soul. O my God, in you I trust' (verses 1, 2).

There is deep intensity and sincerity in this prayer, and it finishes with David asking for his people what he has been praying for himself (verse 22).

Notwithstanding his deep faith, there is evidence that David is depressed:
> 'Turn to me and be gracious to me for I am lonely and afflicted' (verse 16).

He is disturbed and anguished in mind:

> 'Relieve the troubles of my heart, and bring me out of my distress' (verse 17).

He is stricken by a sense of guilt and failure:

> 'Consider my affliction and my trouble, and forgive all my sins' (verse 18).

David begins by addressing God as, 'O Lord' (verse 1), and then moves to the more personal, 'O my God' in verse 2. But he is in great need of a saviour and this is met in verse 5 where he affirms: 'You are the God of my salvation'. What, then, does David actually ask of God? As so often in other psalms, he requests that he may not be defeated and thereby humiliated by his enemies (verse 2). He is also desperately in need of guidance, and is prepared to wait for it (verses 4, 5). Following his recollection of God's covenant love, he is able to face up to his sense of personal failure:

> 'For your name's sake, O Lord, pardon my guilt, for it is great' (verse 11)

And the final prayer for himself is:

> 'Guard my life, and deliver me' (verse 20a).
>
> 'May integrity and uprightness preserve me, for I wait for you' (verse 21).

But David, the King, can never forget his people, and so he concludes his prayer, as he so often does in his psalms, by interceding for the nation.

Psalm 51

We have already looked at the background of this psalm in Chapter 7, and examined David's double sin of adultery and conspiracy to murder. So we know that Psalm 51 is concerned with huge personal problems and with spiritual sickness. David's whole life has been stricken and become dislocated through his sense of guilt (verses 3, 4). Not surprisingly, this psalm has within it the most comprehensive confession of sin in the whole of Scripture. David refers to his guilt in three ways: as 'wrong-doing', that is rebellion, violating God's commandments; as 'iniquity', meaning offence against God's righteousness; and as 'sin', which can be defined as missing the mark or falling short of a fixed standard. David could hardly be painting a darker picture!

But for all this psalm's dark overtones, the light breaks through, as it surely always must, in the heartfelt prayer of a repentant sinner to a gracious and forgiving God. And the last part of the psalm (verses 13-19) resounds with optimism.

But first, there is the coming to God in repentance. David knows that he can pray for mercy only because he senses that God's love is greater than his sin. Because of this confidence he can make a full and frank confession (verses 1-4a). He acknowledges that sin is primarily an offence against God, but that it also has a 'knock-on' effect; every generation has been polluted by its infection (verse 5). The psalmist also realises that God looks for integrity not only in our outward actions but in the secrecy of our private, inner lives (verse 6).

David then progresses from confession to prayer for forgiveness and a fresh start for his life. He knows himself to be contaminated and dirty and so asks for cleansing (verse 7) and the restoring of hope that he will be made whole again (verse 8). He pleads with God to turn and look away from his shameful deeds (verse 9).

David admits that his deepest problem is his distorted inner nature; he longs to have a totally new outlook on life (verse 10).

He knows that the ultimate calamity would be to lose the sense of God's presence (verse 11). And so he asks that his first love for the Lord may be rekindled (verse 12). The 'joy of your salvation' will enable him to communicate the fruits of his personal forgiveness to others (verses 13-17).

Yet again, David remembers his nation as he concludes his prayer (verses 18, 19). It is possible that these last two verses of the psalm have been added later. Either way, the real climax is in the affirmation that the sacrifice acceptable to God is not the offering of an animal in an elaborate ritual, but that of a humble and broken heart:

> 'The sacrifice acceptable to God is a broken spirit;
> a broken and contrite heart, O God, you will not despise' (verse 17).

Psalm 103

It is particularly fitting to study Psalm 103 after Psalm 51. The latter has marked a devastating mid-life crisis for David and now, in Psalm 103, we can observe him in his later years as he looks back over his life. We are seeing a man who has passed through many critical situations and found his God to have been faithful in every one of them.

And so David's prayer overflows with adoration, praise, thanksgiving and affirmation but – significantly — asks for nothing. It is enough for him to delight himself in the eternal grace of the Lord. In fact, the covenant title of 'the Lord' occurs no fewer than eleven times and points to God's everlasting faithfulness.

David pours out adoration and blessing on the Lord himself, on his name, his character and on his very being. He gives thanks to him for all his goodness and the benefits he has received from his hand (verses 1, 2). He singles out at least five areas of need in which God's grace has been lavished upon him personally. He 'forgives' and 'heals' (verse 3); he 'redeems and crowns' (verse 4), and he 'satisfies you with good as long as you live so that your youth is renewed like the eagle's' (verse 5).

There is no identifiable problem to be overcome in this psalm, only continuous thanksgiving for difficulties that have been resolved. There is no other passage in the Old Testament in which sin is more strongly declared to be completely forgiven. Just look at the comprehensiveness of God's pardon:

> 'He does not deal with us according to our sins, nor repay us according to our iniquities. For as the heavens are high above the earth, so great is his steadfast love towards those who fear him; as far as the east is from the west, so far he removes our transgressions from us' (verses 10-12).

The only Old Testament passage that can approach this powerful assurance of pardon is Micah's prophecy that: 'He will again have compassion upon us; he will tread our iniquities under foot. You will cast all our sins into the depths of the sea' (Micah 7:19).

David's prayer now moves to adoration for the Lord's fatherly compassion (verses 13, 14) and eternal love (verses 15-18). It concludes with praise for his sovereignty (verses 19-22).

David is speaking and praying for all his people in this psalm; indeed, he has a vision of the whole of heaven itself caught up in praise. It seems appropriate, therefore, that we should seek to be caught up in the adoration of the heavenly host in the great sanctus:

> Holy, holy, holy Lord,
> God of power and might,

Heaven and earth are full of your glory;
Hosanna in the highest.

Psalm 139

The greater part of this psalm is, in fact, a meditation on God's omniscience. The thought that God can see and hear our every action and spoken word is a rather discomforting one. Even more disturbing is the idea of his being able to search our minds so that every hidden thought and secret motive lies open before him. He understands everything that happens to us with perfect knowledge. he can place every action within the total context of our lives.

David, however, is not the least bit unnerved by this fact; rather, he welcomes it:

'Such knowledge is too wonderful for me; it is so high
I cannot attain it' (verse 6).

'I praise you, for I am fearfully and wonderfully made.
Wonderful are your works; that I know very well' (verse 14).

The only words of petition come at the end of the prayer:

'Search me, O God, and know my heart; test me and
know my thoughts. See if there is any wicked way in
me, and lead me in the way everlasting' (verses 23, 24).

David can pray these words because he has had such an overwhelming experience of God's grace. He understands that everything is known about his life, from beginning to end, and yet he is still accepted and loved. He has come to himself, returned home and placed himself unreservedly into the hands of his compassionate, caring Father God.

At times we can feel lost in the vastness of our universe, or feel ourselves to count for little more than a statistic in a bureaucratic government machine. We seem to be totally insignificant and life almost meaningless. But then we hear again the words:

> 'How weighty to me are your thoughts, O God! How vast is the sum of them! I try to count them – they are more than the sand; I come to the end – I am still with you' (verses 17, 18).

Omniscience and omnipresence are heavy and perhaps intimidating words. David defines them in personal terms: omniscience in verses 1-6 and omnipresence in verses 7-12. And so, because of God's grace we can be sure that we awake every morning in his presence, and that our final awakening will be with Christ himself (verse 18): I am still with you.

These psalms take us into many aspects of prayer. Here are inspired words that we can make our own as we give our personal interpretation to David's thoughts. Here are prayers for guidance (Psalm 5); for vindication in times of difficulty or personal attack (Psalms 5 and 25); for relief in times of depression (Psalms 13 and 25). Here are prayers of repentance and forgiveness, and of joyful expression when pardon is assured (Psalms 25, 51 and 103).

David helps us in our prayers for deliverance from problems, and from enemies (Psalm 25); and for the rekindling of God's love in our lives (Psalm 51). When we feel heavy and dispirited we need only to look at Psalms 103 and 139 to be lifted up to adoration, praise and thanksgiving. And as we trust and enjoy God's steadfast, covenant love (Psalm 25), we can expand our prayers outwards to the wider community and rejoice with all fellow believers.

> 'But let all who take refuge in you rejoice;

let them ever sing for joy.
Spread your protection over them,
so that those who love your name
may exult in you.
For you bless the righteous, O Lord;
you cover them with favour
as with a shield' (Psalm 5:11, 12).

Chapter **twelve**

Paul

We can learn a great deal about Paul's prayers because they form such a natural and integral part of his letters. As he pictures the Christians in the church he is addressing, it seems as if sometimes he cannot help but break out into spontaneous thanksgiving for them. Then, as his letter gets under way, we find that he is moved to pray on their behalf as the needs of that particular church come into his mind.

As we study the wording of Paul's prayers we may wish to use them just as they are – for what better words can we employ than those from the Bible itself? However, in the case of the longer and more involved prayers, I try to pick out one of the main thoughts and concentrate my own prayer on that.

But let's begin with something very familiar:

'The grace of the Lord Jesus Christ, the love of God, and the communion of the Holy Spirit be with all of you' (2 Corinthians 13:13).

This is a prayer which we can be sure most Christians know by heart. No other biblical words are used more frequently in various acts of worship.

The prayer has within it the clearest statement in the whole of the New Testament regarding the relationship between the three Persons of the Trinity. For many of us, the words of the prayer reflect the sequence of our own Christian experience. First, we have a vision of Christ and his glory and his grace and we make our response of faith. Through coming to Christ we are introduced to the love of God the Father who has planned and guided our salvation. And then, together with other Christians, we discover the uniting and energising power of the Holy Spirit through whom we have fellowship with God in Christ day by day.

The grace of the Lord Jesus Christ . . .

Grace is at the heart of everything that Jesus Christ has done for us. With our hymn book open again, let us have a fresh vision of his glory and grace:

> Before the throne of God above
> I have a strong, a perfect plea;
> A great High Priest, whose name is Love,
> Who ever lives and pleads for me.
>
> My name is graven on his hands,
> My name is written on his heart;
> I know that while in heaven he stands
> No tongue can bid me thence depart.
>
> When Satan tempts me to despair,
> And tells me of the guilt within,
> Upward I look, and see him there
> Who made an end of all my sin.

Because the sinless Saviour died,
My sinful soul is counted free;
For God, the Just, is satisfied
To look on him and pardon me.

Behold him there! the risen Lamb!
My perfect, spotless righteousness,
The great unchangeable I AM,
The King of glory and of grace!

One with himself, I cannot die;
My soul is purchased by his blood;
My life is hid with Christ on high,
With Christ, my Saviour and my God.

CHARITIE LEES BANCROFT

. . . the love of God . . .

What can one say in a few words on such a theme? Let us listen to two voices separated in time by hundreds of years. First, from the medieval mystic, Mother Julian:

> 'Some of us believe that God is All-Power and can do all, and that God is All-Wisdom and knows how to do all. But that God is All-love and wants to do all, here we restrain ourselves. And this ignorance hinders most of God's lovers, as I see it.'

The fictional 5-year-old child in *Mr God, This is Anna* by Fynn (Collins) is not so ignorant. Neither is she restrained:

> 'You see, Fynn, people can only love outside and can only kiss outside, but Mister God can love you right inside, and Mister God can kiss you right inside, so it's

different. Mister God ain't like us; we are a little bit like Mister God but not much yet . . . . You see, Fynn, Mister God is different from us because he can finish things and we can't. I can't finish loving you because I shall be dead millions of years before I can finish, but Mister God can finish loving you, and so it's not the same kind of love, is it?'

. . . and the communion of the Holy Spirit . . .

Only by the Holy Spirit is the grace of Christ and love of God made known to us. He breathes upon the word of God and reveals new truths to us. He is the great Communicator who illuminates our minds and warms our hearts. He touches every part of our human lives so that we become new creations. And this transformation is experienced not only personally but corporately, so that the 'communion of the Holy Spirit' is another way of saying that we are part of the Body of Christ. We ought to find it completely natural, therefore, to pray this prayer with our eyes open; and in looking around us and making eye contact with one another, we shall be giving outward expression to the inner meaning of these wonderful words.

Now let us turn to Paul's letter to the Romans.

> 'First, I thank my God through Jesus Christ for all of you, because your faith is proclaimed throughout the world. For God, whom I serve with my spirit by announcing the gospel of his Son, is my witness that without ceasing I remember you always in my prayers, asking that by God's will I may somehow at last succeed in coming to you' (Romans 1:8-10).

Paul is praying for a church that has not been founded by himself; neither, at the time of writing this great letter, does he know it personally. But he can picture how ideally it is placed to be the home base for the next phase of his Gentile mission. How thrilled he must have been to hear that Jesus was being proclaimed in the very centre of world civilisation. No wonder his prayer begins with an expression of heartfelt gratitude to God.

A **prayer** of petition

> O God, end this wishy-washy, lukewarm mumbling religion.
> Lord, set us on fire.
> God of courage, sweep out our painful timidity.
> Make us divinely unafraid.
> Help us to rise, not in fine-sounding words,
> but in deed, in truth, and in power.
> Lord, send us a Pentecost at any cost.
> And begin in us right now.
> The altar is ready.
> The offering is prepared.
> Now, Lord, send the fire.
>
> FRANK LAUBACH

Then, since a visit to Rome is vital to Paul's plans, this becomes the main burden of his prayer. As he looks forward to it he can have no inkling that instead of making the journey there as a free man and in his own time he will – in the event – travel as a prisoner under armed guard. Thus it is that God answers his prayer, but not in the way he expects. Perhaps he finds some consolation in that the journey is made at the Emperor's expense!

This is a good prayer. It starts with thanksgiving and goes on to bring before God a matter of strategic importance to Paul's expanding ministry. In the same way, our petitionary prayers should be balanced with thanksgiving. Just as it was imperative for Paul to seek God's will for the future, so it is for all of us. Finally, we should learn to be prepared for God to answer our prayers in his own way, and not ours!

Towards the end of Paul's letter to the Romans we find one of the most perfect prayers that could ever be conceived. They are words I frequently use as a preface to the blessing at the close of church services:

'May the God of hope fill you with all joy and peace in believing, so that you may abound in hope by the power of the Holy Spirit' (Romans 15:13).

Our God is the God of hope because Jesus has died for us. All that the Son said and did has been vindicated by God the Father, as witnessed by the resurrection and ascension. We now have a 'friend in high places' who intercedes for us. And by the coming of the Holy Spirit the life, presence, power and love of Jesus are released into the world, and we can experience at a personal level the power of his resurrection and live it. Then we know that our past is forgiven, our present transformed and our future assured. Yes, God in Christ is the source of our hope. But he is also characterised by hope, because he never gives up on us. As by faith we embrace that hope, so joy and peace will flow into our lives, and our hope keeps increasing through the influence of the Holy Spirit.

In his book, *The Prayers of the New Testament*, Donald Coggan makes clear that hope is a grace gift:

'. . . this hope is not something which can be worked up

by self-effort which is dependent on a person's psychological make-up. Faith and hope, like prayer itself, are an operation of the Holy Spirit, as also are joy and peace' (page 105).

Our God is for ever the God of hope because he is the God of resurrection from the dead. We live in that hope.

This is a wonderful prayer to use for those known to us who are passing through a difficult time in their lives; for those in the darkness of depression; for those facing terminal illness; for the lonely and the bereaved. Indeed, in the words of the 1662 *Book of Common Prayer*, 'for all sorts and conditions of men'.

Sometimes we may wish to personalise Paul's words as we pray that our own faith will be strengthened:

'May the God of hope fill me with all joy and peace in believing, so that I may abound in hope by the power of the Holy Spirit.'

Paul's first letter to the Corinthians contains his shortest prayer, just two words:

Marana tha (1 Corinthians 16:22).

The NRSV translates the Aramaic words 'Marana tha' as 'Our Lord, come!' This is one of the earliest and most universal of Christian prayers. It speaks of the longing for Jesus to return in glory and to gather his people together. It may well have been used each morning as Christians sought to bring before their Lord every aspect of the day ahead of them.

This prayer is still valued today. A school of meditation founded by the Benedictine John Main teaches that it is good to set apart at least twenty-five minutes each day to hold this prayer in the centre of the mind in quiet reflection. The two words can be broken into four syllables to make for an easy breathing rhythm which gives an in-out breath on each of them. The prayer then becomes:

Ma – ra – na – tha

Our Lord come

Of course, if it is more natural to us, we can simply say:

Come, Lord Jesus

But there is a rhyme and rhythm about the Aramaic words which allow them to be quietly repeated in the mind for some time. These are healing words, calming anxiety of mind and tension of body. They can induce a deep peace. For those who find it difficult to put into words what they feel about our Lord Jesus Christ, they can also express the sense of deep longing for him, not only for his final coming in glory, but for his daily presence. 'Come, Lord Jesus . . .'; as we continue in prayer, family, friends and acquaintances will come to mind – as will situations – and we can superimpose the words over them as we long for Christ to come more fully into their lives. 'Come, Lord Jesus.' It is not necessary to add anything else; we are, in effect, praying:

Your name be hallowed

Your reign come

Your will be done

According to Acts 17:1-10, Paul could stay in Thessalonica only for about three weeks before he was driven out of the city by Jewish opponents. This was a very short time to establish a church there and to nurture new converts in the Christian faith and life. A little later, Paul was able to send Timothy back to these new Christians to encourage and teach them.

Paul is now writing from Corinth, and Timothy has just rejoined him with reassuring news about the progress of the Thessalonian church. Paul has been fervently praying for them:

> 'Night and day we pray most earnestly that we may see you face to face and restore whatever is lacking in your faith. Now may our God and Father himself and our Lord Jesus direct our way to you. And may the Lord make you increase and abound in love for one another and for all, just as we abound in love for you. And may he so strengthen your hearts in holiness that you may be blameless before our God and Father at the coming of our Lord Jesus with all his saints' (1 Thessalonians 3:10-13).

This is indeed a poignant prayer. Paul longs to be able to revisit them as there is still so much they don't understand; in faith and Christian experience they are still 'babes in Christ'. His prayer asks for guidance, but in the main that they might increase in love for one another, even as he has such deep love for them. He also longs for them to be strengthened in holiness, no doubt having in mind that the Greek moral climate of the day would make Christian standards and values difficult to uphold. In this respect he is concerned to keep before them the glorious hope of the return of Christ.

Don't let's miss the 'for all' (verse 12). Paul does not want his new friends to become a 'holy huddle' in the midst of an alien world. Rather, he prays that they will reach out to share the love of God with all around them.

This is a prayer prayed with emotion – even passion. Prayer driven by real feeling will always be more effective than the mere recitation of beautifully crafted prayers by a dutiful but bored petitioner. And what higher grace gifts can we pray for our friends than that they may abound in love and be strengthened in holiness?

Paul's two prayers from the letter to the Ephesians make a fitting climax to this chapter. In this letter we have two of the greatest prayers in the New Testament. Let's try to imagine the scene as Paul dictates to his secretary the letter he's sending to the capital city in the Roman province of Asia. I can picture him thinking on his feet as he paces the room in his temporary home in Rome where he is under house arrest. He will be held there for about two years while waiting to be called before the highest Roman court in the land to answer a charge of causing a riot in Jerusalem. His prayer made in a letter to the church in Rome to be allowed to visit them had been answered in an unexpected way. Reliably informed of a plot to assassinate him in Palestine, Paul had used his prerogative as a Roman citizen and appealed to the Emperor to try his case.

Under house arrest, he would have been able to entertain visitors but not be free to move beyond his house. Denied any opportunity for missionary activity, Paul can still pray, and reflect deeply about his faith. And as he writes his letter to Ephesus, his spirit soars heavenwards. Nowhere else in his writing does he give a higher picture of the glory of Jesus Christ, and the two prayers in this letter show a spiritual exaltation unequalled in the New Testament by any other writer:

> 'I have heard of your faith in the Lord Jesus and your love toward all the saints, and for this reason I do not cease to give thanks for you as I remember you in my prayers. I pray that the God of our Lord Jesus Christ, the Father of glory, may give you a spirit of wisdom and revelation as you come to know him, so that, with the eyes of your heart enlightened, you may know what is the hope to which he has called you, what are the riches

of his glorious inheritance among the saints, and what is the immeasurable greatness of his power for us who believe, according to the working of his great power. God put this power to work in Christ when he raised him from the dead and seated him at his right hand in the heavenly places, far above all rule and authority and power and dominion, and above every name that is named, not only in this age but also in the age to come. And he has put all things under his feet and has made him the head over all things for the church, which is his body, the fullness of him who fills all in all' (Ephesians 1:15-23).

In such a profusion of powerful words and uplifting images it is not easy to pick out the heart of Paul's prayer, but I believe the key lies in the words, 'with the eyes of your heart enlightened'. Paul is speaking of truths that have not been discovered by human searching or by the use of his brilliant intellect. He has come to understand these things because they have been revealed to him. God has enlightened his heart and mind with new spiritual understanding and now he prays that his friends at Ephesus will have that same experience. Only then, when the 'spirit of wisdom and revelation' has come upon them, will their personal relationship with Christ enable the Holy Spirit to flood their minds with a living hope concerning the inheritance laid up for them in the future. They will also discover that a new power is at work in their lives, none other than the resurrection power of Christ released through the Holy Spirit. The name of Jesus speaks of his present status and authority in heaven, and at this name every knee must bend (see Philippians 2:9-10 which was also probably written at Rome). Even though Jesus is so highly exalted, he is linked spiritually with us all through the church which is his body, as he is its head.

The reference in verse 20 to Jesus' being seated at the right hand of God gives Paul the foundation on which to build this truth in chapter 2.

> 'But God, who is rich in mercy, out of the great love with which he loved us even when we were dead through our trespasses, made us alive together with Christ – by grace you have been saved – and raised us up with him and seated us with him in the heavenly places in Christ Jesus, so that in the ages to come he might show the immeasurable riches of his grace in kindness towards us in Christ Jesus' (Ephesians 2:4-7).

Even now, seated with Christ! Of course, we can know this spiritual truth only through faith, but as 'the eyes of our spirit are enlightened' nothing could give us greater confidence and encouragement in prayer.

Perhaps we should read this second prayer from Ephesians once a week – even try to memorise these verses:

> 'For this reason I bow my knees before the Father, from whom every family in heaven and on earth takes its name. I pray that, according to the riches of his glory, he may grant that you may be strengthened in your inner being with power through his Spirit, and that Christ may dwell in your hearts through faith, as you are being rooted and grounded in love. I pray that you may have the power to comprehend, with all the saints, what is the breadth and length and height and depth, and to know the love of Christ that surpasses knowledge, so that you may be filled with all the fullness of

God. Now to him who by the power at work within us is able to accomplish abundantly far more than all we can ask or imagine, to him be glory in the church and in Christ Jesus to all generations, forever and ever, Amen' (Ephesians 3:14-21).

Again we may ask, given the complexity of this prayer, 'What is the key petition?' Personally, I think it comes in verse 19, 'that you may be filled with all the fullness of God'. As earlier in this letter, Paul prays that they may be strengthened in their 'inner being with power through his Spirit'. The 'fullness of God' he is emphasising here is the fullness of divine love – indescribably and infinitely rich.

Paul prays with intensity, interceding on his knees. Since the normal prayer posture for a Jew would be a standing one, we have an indication here of the depths of his emotion. The only recorded instance of Jesus' kneeling in prayer is in the Garden of Gethsemane (Luke 22:41).

Paul's prayer ends with a doxology (verses 20, 21), a summing up in adoration of all that has gone before. Donald Coggan writes:

> 'When Paul's language soars highest (as in this passage), he is struggling to put into words some tremendous spiritual experience which defies expression. These verses are an attempt to express, in doxological form, the profound truth of the power of Christ available to men, through faith, by his Spirit in the Church. This is the source at once of his Christian character and of his missionary activity. "The Spirit of him who raised up Jesus from the dead" is dwelling in him, giving new life to his mortal body – this is the new principle which

transforms life (cp. Romans 8:11). It is, to appropriate some words found at the end of Pope John's *Journal of a Soul* (page 450), "the humble prayer of a Christian, who thinks of sin but is aware of forgiveness, thinks of death but with a heart that is sure of resurrection, knows the magnitude of his own unworthiness but knows even better the greater magnitude of the Lord's mercy".

"To him be glory!"' (ibid, pages 135, 136).

If Paul's central thought in this prayer is that we should be filled with all the fullness of God, it is helpful to have in mind some words which Hugh Redwood quotes in one of his books:

'Prayer is the grateful acceptance of the good which eternally belongs to you.'

Our heavenly Father wants only our highest good; and when we pray to be filled with all the fullness of God we are in tune with all his gracious purposes for us.

> 0 fill me with thy fullness, Lord,
> Until my very heart o'erflow
> In kindling thought and glowing word,
> Thy love to tell, thy praise to show
>
> **FRANCES RIDLEY HAVERGAL**

In his prayers Paul encourages us in many different ways. He shows us how to pray for God's overruling guidance in our daily lives, and for the help and strength that we constantly need. From his example we learn how to pray, in love, for others. He teaches us to make thanksgiving an integral part of prayer. As we look forward to the coming of Christ, and strive to live blameless lives, all too conscious of our inner needs, he encourages us to pray for the spiritual qualities of hope, joy and peace. Paul's prayers can stimulate within us the desire to know more of the love of Jesus which is beyond human understanding. And so, ending as we began, our prayers are for a deeper experience of the grace of Christ, the love of our heavenly Father and the unifying communion of the Holy Spirit.

Chapter **thirteen**

Parables

There is little doubt that Luke has a special interest in prayer. This is evidenced by the frequency with which he features this theme in his gospel. As we have already seen, Jesus taught widely on the subject, both by word and by the example of his own practice. However, only three of the many parables which have come down to us are directly related to prayer and Luke is alone in recording them. Two of these parables illustrate the same point, which suggests that he is keen to emphasise that particular teaching of Jesus. Each of the stories is full of human interest: one is a colourful domestic drama, the other a scandalous tale of social injustice.

The parable given in Luke 11:5-13 is sometimes entitled, 'The friend at midnight', and it has as its background the eastern custom of providing hospitality to travellers. The story starts with a man arriving in a town late one evening and wondering where he can spend the night. He makes his way to the house of a friend and asks if he can be accommodated. However inconvenient this imposition might be, the eastern hospitality code guarantees that he is made welcome. After a day's journey he is very hungry, but because his arrival is totally unexpected his host has nothing to put before him. He therefore seeks help from a neighbour who, understandably enough, isn't best pleased to be knocked up so late at night. We have already discussed the sleeping arrangements in the average Palestinian home; and so can appreciate that if someone moves off the sleeping platform the whole family is disturbed. Nevertheless, the man whose cupboard is bare cannot afford to be put off. He continues knocking until the householder, accepting that his entire family has been aroused by the commotion anyway, hands over the requested loaves.

The second parable (Luke 18:1-8) concerns just two characters – a widow who has a grievance against a third party, and a judge who 'neither feared God nor had respect for people' (2). The widow asks for justice but her plea falls on deaf ears. The judge refuses even to consider her case. As a widow she has no one to take up her cause, but she is made of too stern a stuff than to be put off. She will not take 'No' for an answer and continues to wear him down with her pleading until, eventually, he can no longer tolerate her nagging and says to himself, 'Though I have no fear of God and no respect for anyone, yet because this widow keeps bothering me, I will grant her justice, so that she may not wear me out by continually coming' (4, 5).

The disturbing factor in this story is the ground on which judgement is ultimately given in favour of the widow. For it has nothing to do with the rightness of her claim, but rather the desire of a corrupt and irritable judge to be rid of her.

These two parables make the same points about prayer. The first is that God is the exact opposite of the reluctant neighbour and the godless judge. Only after much pressurising and cajoling do they eventually – and with bad grace – give what is asked of them. Our heavenly Father, on the other hand, is always ready to hear and answer and to meet our need. Jesus makes this point powerfully when he says:

> 'So I say to you, Ask, and it will be given to you; search, and you will find; knock, and the door will be opened for you. For everyone who asks receives, and everyone who searches finds, and for everyone who knocks, the door will be opened. Is there anyone among you who, if your child asks for a fish, will give a snake instead of a fish? Or if the child asks for an egg, will give a scorpion? If you then, who are evil, know how to give good gifts to your children, how much more will the heavenly Father give the Holy Spirit to those who ask him!' (Luke 11:9-13).

Here Jesus is using one of the ancient principles of logic: if something is true at one level, how much more will it be true at a higher level. If we being human, fallible – even 'evil' – know how to give good gifts to our own children, how much more will the all-wise, all-loving heavenly Father give even better gifts to his spiritual children, right up to the best gift of all, the Holy Spirit? This brings to mind again Archbishop Trench's aphorism, 'Prayer is not overcoming God's reluctance, it is laying hold of his highest willingness.'

Each of these parables makes the same secondary point about prayer which we should note carefully. Both showed that human persistence was called for in seeking satisfaction. We must understand that although God can never be badgered into granting our requests we are, nonetheless, urged to be persistent – 'Jesus told them a parable about their need to pray always and not lose heart' (Luke 18:1).

Perseverance is necessary when our prayers are not answered as quickly as we would wish. Remember, we can see only part of the picture, whereas God sees the whole. What may seem simple requests to us may in fact be rather more complex. It may be the case that a complicated sequence of events has to be worked through before our problems can be resolved or the desires of our hearts fulfilled. As we wait, we need to remain quietly confident and persevere. While we do so, it will be helpful to make prayers of thanksgiving as we affirm that our heavenly Father is working from his side of our problem, and that we are still trusting Him with the outcome. Of course, we need to recognise that our all-wise, all-knowing God may see the situation rather differently from ourselves.

Even if we cannot see any reasons, humanly speaking, why we should have to wait for answers to what we consider straightforward requests, we must still 'not lose heart', as Jesus says. God wants only to bless us, he wants to 'give good things to those who ask him!' (Matthew 7:11). In the 'silence' he may be prompting us to examine our motives or rethink our priorities. He may be seeking to deepen our faith or increase our knowledge of himself and his ways. We have everything to gain.

We couldn't find a better illustration of Jesus' teaching about this aspect of prayer than the one given in Matthew 15. The parables of 'The friend at midnight' and the 'Importunate widow', as the latter is sometimes called, make a perfect backdrop for the true story of a Canaanite woman who came to Jesus with an urgent request. These parables and the true story have points in common: each is about real need (of bread, justice, healing); about dogged persistence and a refusal to be put off in the face of discouragement and rejection; and each has a happy ending!

The story we're looking at is in Matthew 15:21-28 and it prompts us to ask why God is sometimes silent when we pray; why is there no response? There may be many answers to that question, but our examination of this particular incident gives us just one, but one which is extremely important.

Jesus and his disciples have just experienced a very stressful period of ministry. Apart from the usual teaching and healing, there has been sharp controversy with the Pharisees and scribes. Jesus is probably desperately tired and wants to get away for a short break with his friends. So he takes them outside Galilee and into Gentile territory around the important seaport of Tyre. Away from Jewish pressures he is hoping for a period of recreation and the opportunity to give his disciples more specialised teaching. In the event, his holiday doesn't last long. A local woman recognises Him and approaches Him with a serious family problem. Matthew describes the scene:

> 'A Canaanite woman from that region came out and started shouting, "Have mercy on me, Lord, Son of David; my daughter is tormented by a demon"' (15:22).

She is no ordinary Gentile, for her designation of Jesus as 'Son of David' shows a remarkable understanding of who he is. In fact, she is more perceptive than many of her Jewish contemporaries. With such human need on one hand and potential faith on the other, most of us would expect Jesus to have replied: 'Of course I will help you', and followed this with an immediate prayer for healing for her stricken daughter. However, this does not happen. Even more puzzling, Jesus neither answers her nor gives any indication that he has even heard her.

There is a hint in this account that the woman continues for some time with her attempts to get Jesus' attention. Eventually, the disciples can bear it no longer and beg Jesus to 'send her away, for she keeps shouting after us' (15:23).

Here we have a mother with a very sick daughter who comes to Jesus for help. It is a reasonable request and she clearly has

> ### A **prayer** for prayerfulness
>
> Our heavenly Father,
> who through thy Son Jesus Christ
> hast said that men ought always to pray and not to faint,
> we beseech thee, teach us to pray.
> Our spirit is willing but our flesh is weak.
> Give us grace each day to approach thy throne and seek thy face;
> to be concerned as much for thy glory as for our need;
> and in everything by prayer and supplication with thanksgiving
> to make our requests known to thee,
> until all our lives be gathered up into thy presence
> and every breath is prayer.
> Through Jesus Christ our Lord.
> JOHN R. W. STOTT (1921-)

respect for Jesus. In response he says and does absolutely nothing. This is completely out of character and we can find no other examples in the gospels where Jesus acts in this way. He doesn't even apologise or explain, 'I'm on holiday; please come back next week.' He just remains silent and seemingly impervious to her pleading. We are bound to ask, 'What is going on here?'

Jesus' reply to his disciples suggests that the woman is not going to receive any help from Him at all: 'I was sent only to the lost sheep of the house of Israel' (15:24). Can Jesus really be categorically stating that he, the Jewish Messiah, has come to help and save only the Jewish nation? Did Gentile outsiders have no place in his plan or concern?

The story moves on, for at this point the mother grows quiet; her pleading stops and she comes right up to Jesus and, kneeling down at his feet, she says, 'Lord, help me' (15:25). We rightly sense that something has changed as there is a marked difference in her tone. Surely Jesus will now help her as she kneels before him! But no, he is still unyielding. Indeed, his next statement might well have struck dread into the woman's heart. For the first time he addresses her personally: 'It is not fair to take the children's food and throw it to the dogs' (15:26).

Jesus is making it quite clear to her that, as the Jewish 'Son of David' Messiah, his purpose is to feed the children of Israel. He wants her to understand that as a Gentile she has no claim to that food at all. Jews of that day used a variety of terms to express their scorn for Gentiles, 'dogs' being one of the more polite. So what does the despairing mother do next? Slink away in abject disappointment? Lose control and verbally lash Jesus in a hysterical rage? Not a bit of it! What she, in fact, said has come down to us as one of the greatest statements of faith and spiritual insight in the history of Christianity. Some commentators commend her for her wit; and at one level there is humour in her riposte as she seizes upon the image which Jesus is projecting, a scenario familiar to all parents who have endured the messy results of their little darlings' early attempts at self-feeding. But far from being merely witty, her answer is profoundly perceptive. In one sentence she goes to the heart of the relationship between ourselves and almighty God. She has had a moment of revelation in which she realises that everything is of God's grace. She says to Jesus, 'Yes, Lord, yet even the dogs eat the crumbs that fall from their masters' table' (15:27). She is making the point that although adults do not throw their food around as young children do when they eat, inevitably a few crumbs will end up on the floor to be devoured by the pet dog. She may be a Gentile 'dog', but she reckons there are still 'crumbs' of grace from Jesus' table that are sufficient for her and her daughter. Thus she reveals that she has come to an understanding of what she is asking for, and from whom she is seeking it. Jesus is now able to respond to her positively: 'Woman, great is your faith! Let it be done for you as you wish'. And Matthew adds, 'And her daughter was healed instantly' (15:28).

This story teaches us a vital lesson about prayer. A mother came to Jesus with a petition. She was genuinely in need and she came to the right person. So why was there no response? it would seem as if the manner of her asking caused a spiritual blockage. It was suggested in Chapter 11 that emotional outbursts from the psalmists are on occasions understandable, even excusable. But there is something about this woman's approach to Jesus that implies an entirely wrong attitude. She started out by shouting at Jesus. None of us can come to God shouting, petulantly demanding his immediate attention. If we do come before Him in this manner, we should not be surprised if there is no response to our pleading. It was only when the woman came and knelt in the dust before Jesus that the situation began to change. The simple broken words, 'Lord, help me', reflected her new attitude of heart. She began to understand that she could only come to Him trusting in his mercy; her strident demands had achieved nothing. Although Jesus seemed to have been rather severe in his treatment of her, he was simply testing her to see if her apparent change of heart was genuine.

All prayer is of God's grace and mercy. This is why it is such a priceless gift and privilege. Mercy, privilege and gift are grace words which lie at the heart of prayer. Prayer leads us into God's peace because grace is at its centre. It has been said that 'grace is God giving us what we don't deserve; mercy is God not giving us what we do deserve; and peace comes when we live in God's mercy and grace'.

We can only come to God trusting in his grace. This fascinating story shows how one person came to Jesus and learned, rather painfully, that God is the God of all grace.

We move on now to look at another prayer parable recorded by Luke, the one known as 'The tax collector and the Pharisee' (Luke 18:9-14). Jesus' satirical portrayal of a Pharisee at prayer is masterly. First he is shown as ostentatiously 'standing by himself' in the middle of the temple court. He then makes a prayer which admittedly starts with God but then proceeds to use the personal pronoun consistently in a eulogy of self-righteous virtue. He elevates himself far above his fellow men in a proud rush of moral self-congratulation.

I find myself joining in the usual criticism of him for his blinkered spiritual pride. But it is just at this point that I begin to feel uncomfortable. In my endeavour to grasp fully the judgement Jesus is making, I suddenly realise that I am in the parable. As I condemn the Pharisee, I see that I am just like him! In my self-righteous pride I hear myself saying that I could never pray 'like that'. It is disturbing to face the truth about myself, and see that the only way in which I can identify with the tax collector and pray, 'God be merciful to me, a sinner', as he did is by first acknowledging that I am the Pharisee: that I am judging him in precisely the same way he judged the tax collector.

How the word of God penetrates to the very heart and centre of our being!

> 'The word of God is living and active, sharper than any two-edged sword, piercing until it divides soul from spirit, joints from marrow; it is able to judge the thoughts and intentions of the heart. And before him no creature is hidden, but all are naked and laid bare to the eyes of the one to whom we must render an account' (Hebrews 4:12, 13).

The writer of the letter to the Hebrews has clearly been influenced by Psalm 139 which we studied in the last chapter.

There is, however, more to say about this parable. It is the inspiration for one of the best-known prayers of the universal Church, possibly the most popular after the Lord's Prayer and the 'Grace' (2 Corinthians 13:13). The 'Jesus prayer' comes from the Eastern Church and is extremely brief. It opens in affirmation of Jesus and concludes with the plea of the tax collector in the Temple. The prayer has come down to us in slightly different forms, the best-known version possibly being:

> Lord Jesus, Son of God, have mercy on me a sinner.

My personal preference is to give it greater depth of meaning by adding two words. The prayer then becomes:

> Lord Jesus *Christ*, Son of God, *Saviour*, have mercy on me a sinner.

Every word of this prayer has significance. It begins by giving the second Person of the Trinity the title 'Lord' which speaks of divinity. We next use the personal name of 'Jesus' as we think of his total identification with us in his humanity. Finally, 'Christ' speaks to us of Jesus as Messiah, the one who fulfilled all the expectations of the Old Testament.

These three opening titles are now summed up in words which express who he is and what he did. 'Son of God' represents all that our Lord Jesus Christ is in his divinity. And 'Saviour' epitomises all that Jesus came to do in his perfect humanity: his life poured out in service and laid down as a sacrifice for the salvation of the world.

To this point it has been a prayer of affirmation and adoration. Now it moves into petition:

> Have mercy on me a sinner.

As we view the glory of the holy Son of God, the bleeding, suffering Man on the cross, what other prayer could we make?

Even today this prayer, which has come down to us over the centuries, has lost none of its power. The Russian holy men breathed it continually as they went about the business of their daily lives. Clearly, they found it to be a source of strength. And so for ourselves, too, it is a prayer we can use at any time and in any place. Just to breathe it silently, even in the midst of the day's busy activity, will be to open ourselves to the grace of God and find our hearts warmed, our spirits calmed and our faith strengthened.

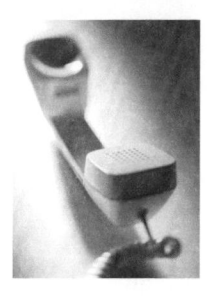

Chapter **fourteen**

Pathfinders

I should now like to own a debt of gratitude to some of the 'pathfinders' who have guided me in my understanding and practice of prayer. In introducing them, I hope that the quotations from their teaching may lead you to a richer experience in your own prayer life.

In my days as a young Christian I remember wandering round a bookshop looking for a book on prayer. In my ignorance I didn't know where to start. In the event, the book I chanced upon could not have been a better one for a beginner. Although I cannot recall its title, I remember that the author was Ronald Sinclair; his name meant nothing to me but the subtitle caught my attention. It stated that the method of prayer described in the book was that taught by G. A. Studdert Kennedy, a name which was familiar to me because he had been a well-known and popular World War I army chaplain known to the troops as 'Woodbine Willie'.

It was Studdert Kennedy who first encouraged me to use my imagination in prayer: to picture Christ's presence, and to visualise his touching and changing human lives. You will have seen earlier in this book that I introduced this dimension of prayer – proof of this man's lasting influence upon me.

Probably the next book to impact upon my prayer life was *Prayer*, by the Norwegian writer O. Hallesby. One chapter in particular, on the theme of wrestling in prayer, has remained with me. The biblical background was the story of Jacob's wrestling all night with the angel of the Lord before his fateful encounter with his brother Esau (Genesis 32:24-30). It taught me to be patient in prayer, to persevere and to recognise that there are spiritual forces at work, trying to divert me from my purpose. Perhaps the greatest truth I learned was that God wants to release his blessing upon us the moment he sees that we are really serious in asking for it.

A **prayer** of acknowledgement

> Prayer projects faith on God, and God on the world
> Only God can move mountains,
> but faith and prayer move God.
> E. M. BOUNDS (1835-1913)

Later when I was preparing for the ordained ministry, I came across a small book entitled, *Power through Prayer*, by a London minister. In this, E. M. Bounds tells the story of his church and his despair at being unable to see any true spiritual life. In his discouragement he bought a copy of the parliamentary voters' list covering his parish and began to pray for each person on it by name, giving two or three hours each day to this task. The book recounts the amazing transformation that took place in his parish. As all other factors were unchanged, E. M. Bounds firmly believed that this was due to God's moving in the lives of the people for whom he so patiently and faithfully interceded. As I have moved from parish to parish during my ministry, one of the first things I have done is to avail myself of an Electoral List!

E. M. Bounds taught me that prayer lists have real value. Of course, they need to be handled with caution. Clearly, it is good to have an *aide-memoire* so that we don't overlook people and situations that need our prayers; but as soon as such lists lead us into heavy, dutiful, legalistic prayer, they should be reviewed, even discontinued for a period of time.

Archbishop Anthony Bloom, one-time Metropolitan of Sourozh, a man steeped in the Russian Orthodox tradition, wrote a book which has helped me greatly; it is entitled, *School for Prayer*, and the following extract gives us his thoughts on morning prayer:

> 'Awake in the morning and the first thing you do, thank God for it, even if you don't feel particularly happy about the day which is to come. "This day which the Lord has made, let us rejoice and be grateful in it." Once you have done this, give yourself time to realise the truth of what you are saying and really mean it – perhaps on the level of deep conviction and not of what one might call exhilaration. And then get up, wash, clean, do whatever else you have to do, and then come to God again. Come to God again with two convictions. The one is that you are God's own and the other is that this day is also God's own, it is absolutely new,

absolutely fresh. It has never existed before . . . it is like a vast expanse of unsoiled snow. No one has trodden on it yet. It is all virgin and pure in front of you. And now, what comes next? What comes next is that you ask God to bless this day, that everything in it should be blessed and ruled by him. After that you must take it seriously, because very often one says "O God bless me", and having got the blessing we act like the prodigal son – we collect all our goods and go to a strange country to lead a riotous life.

'This day is blessed by God, it is God's own and now let us go into it. You walk in this day as God's own messenger; whoever you meet, you meet in God's own way. You are there to be the presence of the Lord God, the presence of Christ, the presence of the Spirit, the presence of the Gospel – this is your function on this particular day . . . every person you meet is a gift of God, every circumstance you will meet is a gift of God, whether it is sweet or bitter, whether you like or dislike it. It is God's own gift to you and if you take it that way, then you can face any situation. But then you must face it with the readiness that anything may happen, whether you enjoy it or not, and if you walk in the name of the Lord through a day which has come fresh and new out of his own hands and has been blessed for you to live with it, then you can make prayer and life really like two sides of one coin. You act and pray in one breath, as it were, because all the situations that follow one another require God's blessing' (pages 46, 47).

For those of us who have a problem with early-morning prayer,

I recount Anthony Bloom's story of an elderly Russian woman who had great difficulty in praying. Nothing seemed to work for her. She just could not experience any sense of Christ's presence, let alone talk to him. She was counselled to be silent before God, rather than to talk all the time: 'Just sit, look around . . . then take up your knitting and for fifteen minutes knit before the face of God . . . just knit and try to enjoy the peace of your room.' So she started, and Anthony Bloom quotes her own words:

> 'I felt so quiet because the room was so peaceful. There was a clock ticking but it didn't disturb the silence, its ticking just underlined the fact that everything was so still and after a while I remembered that I must knit before the face of God, and so I began to knit. And I became more and more aware of the silence. The needles hit the arm-rest of my chair, the clock was ticking peacefully, there was nothing to bother about, I had no need of straining myself, and then I perceived that this silence was not simply an absence of noise, but that the silence had substance. It was not absence of something but presence of something. The silence had a density, a richness, and it began to pervade me. The silence around began to come and meet the silence in me . . . . All of a sudden I perceived that the silence was a presence. At the heart of the silence there was him who is all stillness, all peace, all poise' (pages 60, 61).

J. V. Taylor was first a missionary in Africa, then General Secretary of the Church Missionary Society before becoming Bishop of Winchester. He wrote one of the most searching books of recent years on the Holy Spirit, *The Go-Between God*. In the final chapter which he entitled 'Loving', John Taylor writes:

'There are two kinds of prayer . . . which I prefer to call the prayer of stillness and the prayer of movement . . . .

A **prayer** for knowledge

> Thanks be to thee, my Lord Jesus Christ,
> for all the benefits thou has won for me,
> for all the pains and insults thou has borne for me.
> O most merciful Redeemer, Friend and Brother,
> may I know thee more clearly,
> love thee more dearly,
> and follow thee more nearly,
> day by day.
> *RICHARD OF CHICHESTER (1197-1253)*

'The difference does not lie in subject matter but in the way in which one looks at it. It is not that in the prayer of movement we choose to dwell on passages in the Bible or incidents in the life of Christ or the needs of the world, while in the prayer of stillness we seek the vision of God in a direct exposure to the uncreated light. The difference is much simpler than that. In the prayer of movement our mind moves from thought to thought and from image to image as it does most of the time when we are "thinking" either about God or tonight's dinner, an article in the newspaper, or a chapter in the Bible, the Christians in the Sudan or the pack in the Welsh rugby team. But in the prayer of stillness the mind stands still and looks, takes in what is standing before it and gives itself, but does not move from thought to thought.

'I can make this clearer, perhaps, by recalling the distinction . . . between the truth "about" someone or something and the truth "of" someone or something. In the prayer of movement we try to open ourselves to more of the truth "about" Jesus by dwelling on part of the gospel; or to open ourselves to more of the truth "about" the Sudanese church by reading a letter and using our imagination with compassion. In the prayer of stillness we try to hold ourselves open to the impact "of" Jesus not in a succession of bits and pieces, but as one whole person; or, aided by such knowledge as we already have about the Sudan, we try to hold ourselves still before the truth of those Christians "because they are there", open to their reality without thinking any new thoughts about them.'

John V. Taylor, *The Go-Between God*, SCM Press.

I hope you will find that this picture of the 'prayer of stillness' complements what I have already written about it in earlier chapters.

Reginald Somerset Ward was an immensely influential spiritual director in the first half of the twentieth century. Much of his ministry was spent counselling others, among whom were a number of leading churchmen. I include him in my pathfinders because I have found the thoughts in his book *To Jerusalem* particularly helpful. Some of his more profound ideas do not make easy reading and so I offer a close paraphrase of a sample of his teaching on prayer, sometimes drawing on his exact words, but, I trust, never altering the meaning.

Somerset Ward teaches that the origin of all prayer lies in the life and relationship of the Trinity – Father, Son and Holy Spirit. Because God is love, the three persons of the Trinity are eternally expressing this perfect love relationship with each other. The unity of the Godhead is enjoyed in this love. This divine, eternal love is so dynamic that it overflows into God's creation. The universe exists, and we have our being, only because of God's love – that 'infinite stream of the divine love eternally pulsing through the Persons of the Blessed Trinity, out from God, and drawing the world back into God'.

Within that tide of love is to be seen 'both the origin and the cause of prayer. It is because we are caught up by that love that we pray' It follows that the more fully we surrender to that love, the better we will pray.

Every time we pray we are, in fact, 'sharing in, co-operating with, the very life of God.' And the starting point of prayer must be the conscious uniting of ourselves to that 'stream of divine love' which is ever flowing from the love relationship within the Holy Trinity. This is the very heart of prayer. Once we are consciously aware of being enfolded within this divine love, the details of our petitions become much less important. So be quiet, receptive, and open, 'join yourself to the love which is flowing from the Godhead all around you. When you have joined yourself to that love, and will accomplish its desire, draw others into the same stream, ask what seems to fit in with the divine desire, or simply give yourself up to its working.'

Over-anxiety in prayer is an ever-present danger. We often fear the inadequacy of our effort and this tends to 'destroy its spontaneity. . . . When we realise that the stream of divine love is forever carrying us and our desires into God, we are able, by joining it, to relax the tension of our effort . . . we should learn to rely more on the energy of God's desire in prayer and less on our own feeble efforts.'

Somerset Ward died in 1962, but will continue to live in the memory of many men and women who have found that his insights into prayer have enriched their spiritual lives.

I've been encouraged in my praying by people from a wide spectrum of spirituality. Here I have mentioned a celebrated army chaplain, a Norwegian evangelical, a London parish priest, a Russian Orthodox archbishop, an Anglican bishop and an Anglo-Catholic spiritual director. Each one has encouraged and inspired me. I trust each will do the same for you.

Chapter **fifteen**

Power

I believe that the most powerful incentive to prayer is summed up in the simple phrase: 'name of Jesus'. Where there is a living faith in Christ, using the name of Jesus releases spiritual power, and it is this truth that we will be exploring in the final pages of this book.

In the previous chapter we considered Somerset Ward's assertion that the three Persons of the Trinity are the source of every experience of prayer. Divine love is eternally moving outwards to embrace all creation. Let us see how this was a reality in the lives of Jesus' early followers.

In the Acts of the Apostles the expression, 'name of Jesus', occurs only after the coming of the Holy Spirit. It is significant that Jesus had already died, been raised to life and had ascended to heaven before the Holy Spirit could appear in his fullness. When the Son's earthly work was complete, the Spirit came upon his followers on the day of Pentecost so that his mission could be continued.

Soon after this momentous happening, Peter and John find themselves confronted with a lame beggar at the Temple gate.

Peter says to him, 'I have no silver or gold, but what I have I give you; in the name of Jesus Christ of Nazareth, stand up and walk' (Acts 3:6). The lame man immediately jumps up and begins to walk, leaping and praising God in his joy!

The miracle causes such a stir that Peter and John are arrested. In the course of their defence before the Jewish authorities they affirm that the name of Jesus is a healing and a saving name:

> 'This Jesus is "the stone that was rejected by you, the builders; it has become the cornerstone". There is salvation in no one else, for there is no other name under heaven given among mortals by which we must be saved' (Acts 4:11, 12).

Jesus came to bring wholeness and salvation in his name. We may say, then, that the 'name of Jesus' focuses and sums up the power and authority of all his mighty acts. The phrase is a 'code' for the whole of Jesus Christ's saving work.

When we pray in the name of Jesus we are using words of authority which release divine power; as he promised his friends just before he ascended to heaven:

> 'All authority in heaven and on earth has been given to me' (Matthew 28:18).

The authority invested in his name did not, however, derive from Jesus alone but from all three Persons of the Trinity who were active in each of his mighty acts. We see this principle constantly at work in Jesus' life. Within the divine plan of God the Father, the Holy Spirit overshadowed the virgin Mary so that Jesus the Son of God was conceived, and born into our world.

At the Son's baptism by John, the Holy Spirit appeared as a dove and the Father spoke his word of encouragement and approval:

> 'Now when all the people were baptized, and when Jesus also had been baptized and was praying, the heaven was opened, and the Holy Spirit descended upon him in bodily form like a dove. And a voice came from heaven, "You are my Son, the Beloved; with you I am well pleased"' (Luke 3:21, 22).

At the human level all children need the encouragement of parental approval, and the Son of God receives it here from both the Father and the Holy Spirit.

Moving on to the death of Jesus we again see that each Person of the Trinity is involved. When we think of Calvary we tend, inevitably, to concentrate on the physical suffering of the Son, and the spiritual significance of his atoning death. But the Holy Spirit is also present as Jesus offers his life for the sins of the world. The letter to the Hebrews makes this clear:

> 'For if the blood of goats and bulls, with the sprinkling of the ashes of a heifer, sanctifies those who have been defiled so that their flesh is purified, how much more will the blood of Christ, who through the eternal Spirit offered himself without blemish to God, purify our conscience from dead works to worship the living God!' (Hebrews 9:13, 14).

And surely, the Father was involved as Jesus carried through the plan which was in place even 'from the foundation of the world' (Revelation 13:8). It is impossible for us to imagine the agony of the Father as he looked upon the wounded body and scorched mind of his perfect Son. How would any human parent have felt? How much more, God the Father? As we meditate on this aspect of Calvary we will each have our own picture in mind. I find that such imaginings are more easily expressed in poetic form, and my own reflections resulted in these lines:

> God sighed
> cried black cumulo-nimbus tears
> which shuttered the light from the sight
> of the bleeding tree
>
> Amazed
> fazed red-alerted legions averted awed eyes
> from the curtained skies
> dazed by the abba pain
>
> God wept,
> kept the vigil of noon while his beautiful son
> wracked and cracked and whispered, 'Why me?'
>
> God stayed
> dismayed that his primeval plan
> was worse for his man
> had grace been betrayed?
> but how else remade?
>
> God thought
> to abort the mind-scorching torture
> but seeing all future
> bound up in this fracture
> he stayed
> surveyed the arm-stretching son
> like Moses upraised on Amalekite hill
> so still, but within
> his trust, tho' dismayed, has won

> God bore
> the raw Golgotha wound as the man drank the gall
> and shouted to all his victory cry – 'tetelestai!'
> sank his head so peacefully dead
> while the cleansing red
> a salvific sea
> spread from the foot of the tree
> throughout the cursed land
> as planned.

Assuredly, the name of Jesus carries the authority given by the victory of the cross, confirmed by the Father and the Holy Spirit.

That authority is further endorsed by the next mighty act, the resurrection 'according to the working of his great power . . . when he raised him from the dead' (Ephesians 1:19, 20). We have already looked at this marvellous text in chapter 12 but it is worth reading again, including verse 21.

There are personal and life-changing repercussions from the 'immeasurable greatness of his power for us who believe'. For:

> 'If the Spirit of him who raised Jesus from the dead
> dwells in you, he who raised Christ from the dead will
> give life to your mortal bodies also through his Spirit
> that dwells in you' (Romans 8:11).

Picture the inert, cold body of Jesus lying in the tomb very early on Easter morning. There can be no doubt that he really had died on the cross. Then, God breathes his own vitalising power into the dead body and Jesus returns to life. He leaves his grave clothes behind where they had been when wrapped around his body. That is the actual eyewitness report of John and Peter (John 20:3-8). Jesus, alive now in a new and vital way, advances out of the tomb, past the moved stone and into the world.

The Apostles' Creed states that on the third day 'he rose from the dead'. The verb is active. He arose! However, there is also a sense in which he was raised in the plan of the Father through the power of the Holy Spirit. And here is the amazing truth for ourselves: in Romans 8:11 Paul states that the Spirit of holy power which raised Jesus from the dead is the same Spirit who lifts us up as well. And so, when we pray in the name of Jesus we are actually releasing the resurrection power of Jesus Christ into our own lives. I wonder if we truly realise this?

Recently my wife and I flew to Canada to visit her family. She had never been in an aircraft before and I had never flown commercially. Not surprisingly, we had mixed feelings about this new experience. As the plane climbed towards the cruising height of 36,000 feet I reflected on the forces that were at play on the aircraft. The weight of this large jumbo jet must have been many hundreds of tons. The force of gravity was endeavouring to pull us downwards to destruction. But at the same time the thrust of the four great jet engines was lifting us upwards. The down-drag of 'death' was more than counterbalanced by the up-thrust of 'life'. At that moment I suddenly recalled the words of Paul in Romans 8:2:

> 'The law of the Spirit of life in Christ Jesus has set you free from the law of sin and death.'

Here Paul is using the word 'law' in the sense of an active principle which has real power within it. The law, principle or power of sin and death, is always trying to pull us down to destruction. But the other law which is at work is greater. The Spirit of life in Christ Jesus is always at work, lifting us up and raising us to new life. And this is happening every time we pray. The simplest word to God in prayer is releasing divine power – resurrection power – into our lives and the lives of those for whom we pray. However weak, feeble, faltering or pathetic we feel our prayers to be, this is the truth of the situation. Our welcoming abba Father God hears and the resurrection power of Jesus Christ is released within us through the power of the Holy Spirit.

A **prayer** of potency

> The potency of prayer hath subdued the strength of fire;
> it hath bridled the rage of lions, hushed anarchy to rest, extinguished wars,
> appeased the elements, expelled demons, burst the chains of death,
> expanded the gates of heaven, assuaged diseases, repelled frauds,
> rescued cities from destruction, stayed the sun in its course,
> and arrested the progress of the thunderbolt.
> Prayer is an all-sufficient panoply,
> a treasure undiminished, a mine which is never exhausted,
> a sky unobscured by clouds, a heaven unruffled by the storm.
> It is the root, the fountain, the mother of a thousand blessings.
> ST CHRYSOSTOM (C. 347-407)

And there is even more good news. What do you picture Jesus doing at this moment? Perhaps you reply that he has ascended into heaven and is now seated at the right hand of God the Father. Yes, this is absolutely correct. But does this imply that, with his earthly work finished, Jesus is now taking a well-earned rest? Sitting naturally suggests that the task has been completed and that there is nothing more to do. But to think of Jesus as merely resting now and doing nothing except receiving the adulation of the heavenly host is wide of the mark. He is, in reality, continuing his prayer ministry which he began on earth. Just as he daily prayed for his disciples and the crowds that he wished to serve, so now he intercedes for all people universally throughout time until he returns in glory:

> 'He is able for all time to save those who approach God through him, since he always lives to make intercession for them' (Hebrews 7:25).

At this moment in time, Jesus is praying for you and me. He is praying for all for whom we pray. Could we have any greater encouragement in praying? And let's remember that he is praying supremely on the grounds of his atoning death and powerful resurrection. He is praying to his Father; and the Holy Spirit, who now represents him universally on earth, is releasing his life into our world. Hence it is still a fully Trinitarian activity.

What a joy to know that we have a Friend in high places who understands all about the real difficulties and conditions of our daily lives and can interpret them sensitively as we approach God the Father through him. Yes, Jesus Christ is our great High Priest and he is praying for us continually. But we haven't yet exhausted the good news, because there are even further grounds for encouragement. As well as God the Son's interceding for us, God the Holy Spirit is actually praying within us. The prepositions are so important. Christ *for* us: Holy Spirit *in* us. He knows how faltering our prayers can be. He recognises our difficulties in even beginning to pray. He understands our problems in finding the right words to express ourselves. And he is present, at the deepest level of our being, guiding, prompting, encouraging and praying within us. Naturally we wonder: how can we be sure? Paul gives the answer:

'Likewise the Spirit helps us in our weakness; for we do not know how to pray as we ought, but that very Spirit intercedes with sighs too deep for words. And God, who searches the heart, knows what is the mind of the Spirit, because the Spirit intercedes for the saints according to the will of God' (Romans 8:26, 27).

As we recognise here the activity of all three Persons of the Trinity, we realise that prayer is not so much a human activity as a supernatural work in us. As Martin Luther said:

'All that the man, or the spirit within him, can manage is a little sound and a feeble groaning as, "Ah! Father!" and the Father understands – a simple vocative without expression and connection is established.'

After all, a baby crying does not use words but the mother understands. In his *Letters to Malcolm*, C. S. Lewis quotes these lines by an unknown author:

They tell me, Lord, that when I seem
To be in speech with you,
Since but one voice is heard, it's all a dream,
One talker aping two.

Sometimes it is, yet not as they
Conceive it. Rather, I
Seek in myself the things I hoped to say,
But lo, my wells are dry.

Then, seeing me empty, you forsake
The listener's role and through
My dumb lips breathe and into utterance wake
The thoughts I never knew.

And thus you neither need reply
Nor can; thus, while we seem
Two talkers, Thou art One forever, and I
No dreamer, but thy dream.

The power and victory that radiate from Christ's cross, resurrection and heavenly intercession are now focused for us in the name of Jesus. His name sums up all that he is in his incarnate life, his atoning death and his enthronement in heaven. Through the encouragement of the Holy Spirit we have confidence to use that name with the authority that God has given it.

Often, a helpful way to use the name of Jesus is in a simple prayer of praise. Praise is always a powerful form of prayer: simply praising God for all that he is and has done for us – regardless of what our personal circumstances are at the time. Perhaps, at its simplest, we are praising Jesus because he is alive and he is Lord. Sometimes our circumstances make praise difficult. How can we praise God when we are experiencing depression within or disasters around us?

Merlin C. Carothers helped many people in his book *From Prison to Praise*. I quote a passage from it which shows the heart of his message:

> 'Jesus didn't promise to change the circumstances around us, but he did promise great peace and pure joy to those who would learn to believe that God actually controls things.
>
> 'The very act of praise releases the power of God into a set of circumstances and enables God to change them if this is his design. Very often it is our attitudes that hinder the solution of a problem. God is sovereign

and could certainly cut across our wrong thought patterns and attitudes. But his perfect plan is to bring each of us into fellowship and communion with himself and so he allows circumstances and incidents which will bring our wrong attitudes to our attention.

'I have come to believe that the prayer of praise is the highest form of communion with God, and one that always releases a great deal of power into our lives – praising him is not something we do because we feel good; rather it is an act of obedience. Often the prayer of praise is done in sheer teeth-gritting will power; yet when we persist in it, somehow the power of God is released into us and into the situation, first in a trickle perhaps, but later in a growing stream that finally floods us and washes away the hurts and scars.'

As I try to focus the power of the name of Jesus in my own prayers I often use an affirmation that is based on the words of Paul which we looked at in an earlier chapter (Pattern):

'Who will separate us from the love of Christ? Will hardship, or distress, or persecution, or famine, or nakedness, or peril, or sword ? . . . No, in all these things we are more than conquerors through him who loved us' (Romans 8:35, 37).

We can take hold of this truth in our regular prayer time, or at any moment of the day or night, using the simple words:

Jesus

More than conquerors

Through your love.

Repeat these words quietly, slowly and with total confidence: they speak of Christ's final authority over the whole of life.

They carry with them the assurance of his victory, for:

> 'At the name of Jesus every knee should bend, in heaven and on earth and under the earth, and every tongue should confess that Jesus Christ is Lord, to the glory of God the Father' (Philippians 2:10, 11).

The authority that is vested in Jesus is powerfully manifested in the story of the storm on the sea of Galilee. Jesus, exhausted after a heavy day of ministry, asks his disciples to sail across to the quiet of the eastern shore. A sudden squall arises and the experienced fishermen see that the boat is about to be swamped. Jesus, deeply asleep in the stern, is roughly awakened by the terrified disciples and quickly takes in the situation. At once, he commands wind and water:

> 'Peace! Be still!' (Mark 4:39)

Straight away, the storm subsides and all is calm. From the disciples' viewpoint the situation had been totally out of control, but the moment they brought the problem to Jesus his powerful authority restored control and safety.

It is helpful to recall this thrilling incident whenever we feel afraid or overwhelmed by our circumstances. We all have times in our lives when a situation can seem out of control – just as it seemed for the disciples caught up in that sudden, life-threatening storm. We feel utterly helpless as we turn to the Lord in prayer. And what better words could we use than, 'Lord, save us'? As we hand our problem over to him, we hear his word of authority as he speaks into our situation: 'Peace! Be still'. As we trust his word of power we allow his calm to pervade us. And – because Jesus Christ is always greater than our problem – we affirm his lordship:

> Save us, Lord,

> Peace! Be Still!
> All is calm
> Jesus is Lord.

My hope is that this brief journey into prayer has made us mindful above everything else that all is of grace.

This has been a constantly recurring theme as we've first acknowledged the incredible privilege we have in prayer. We've looked objectively at our preparation, and one or two of the problems that most of us experience in our devotional lives. We've explored the benefits of meditation in deepening our sense of God's presence, and we've touched on prayer for wholeness. We've seen something of the breadth and the power of the Lord's Prayer, and its potential for widening the scope of our personal petitions. Inspiration and encouragement have come to us from both Old and New Testament saints and hopefully – for some at least – from twentieth-century writers.

Finally, we have tried to learn the secret of victorious prayer and how we may hold ourselves in the stream of resurrection power that flows from Christ's empty tomb and heavenly intercession.

And we have only just begun! We are all too aware of our ignorance, our inexperience, our emptiness. But we take heart and our encouragement is in the God of all grace. In truth, every act of worship glorifies God; every affirmation of praise radiates Christ's resurrection life into the world; and every expression of prayer releases the love of God in us, renewing and transforming our lives. Prayer, ultimately, is tapping the infinite resources we have in Jesus our Lord – 'the riches of his grace that he lavished on us' (Ephesians 1:7, 8).

Thou hidden source of calm repose,
Thou all-sufficient love divine,
My help and refuge from my foes,
Secure I am, if thou art mine:
And lo, from sin, and grief, and shame,
I hide me, Jesus, in thy name.

Thy mighty name salvation is,
And keeps my happy soul above;
Comfort it brings, and power, and peace,
And joy, and everlasting love;
To me, with thy dear name, are given
Pardon, and holiness, and heaven.

Jesus, my all in all thou art:
My rest in toil, my ease in pain,
The med'cine of my broken heart,
In war my peace, in loss my gain,
My smile beneath the tyrant's frown,
In shame my glory and my crown;

In want my plentiful supply,
In weakness my almighty power,
In bonds my perfect liberty,
My light in Satan's darkest hour,
In grief my joy unspeakable,
My life in death, my heaven in hell.

CHARLES WESLEY